ARCHIGRAPHY

ARCHIGRAPHY
LETTERING ON BUILDINGS

Agnès Laube
Michael Widrig

Birkhäuser

FOREWORD

Building signage brings together two disciplines, architecture and graphic design, in a relationship that is summarized by the term *archigraphy*. In archigraphics, the graphic design constitutes a secondary semiotic layer that should always incorporate its substrate—the architecture. Effective archigraphic designs support the statement made by a building, strengthen its identity, or—deliberately and for good reasons—form a contrast to it.

Designing signage appropriate to a specific building is a complex task. While most people understand the written code involved, they lack the key to understanding the architecture. How can graphic designers learn to "read," understand, and interpret architecture and react to it with their designs? Graphic designers usually work in two dimensions and on small scales and are often not aware of the significance of space. How large should lettering be? What is the nature of the sight lines inside and outside buildings? What sorts of materials can be used for lettering, and how can it be constructed and mounted? Architects, on the other hand, usually have not studied the history of lettering or the typographical applications of fonts.

Our methodology is based on the idea of deriving building signage and wayfinding elements from the architecture to which they relate. We aim to contribute to and explicitly promote the development of a new signage culture by analyzing current designs as well as looking back at the history of archigraphy. The chapter "Learning from History" traces the development of archigraphy from 1900 onward and illustrates it with many examples. Wherever possible, contemporary architecture should be marked with equally contemporary signage. This was a premise already adopted by modernist designers at the beginning of the twentieth century. The new discipline of archigraphy was founded by the architects and typographers of the Neues Bauen (New Building) movement, and some of their (playfully) radical designs still remain groundbreaking today.

The examination of recent projects that makes up the core of this publication focuses on the exciting forms of contemporary signage they have produced. Each of these projects illustrates a strategy for deriving integral signage from an architectural design. "Integral" needs to be understood here in a comprehensive sense, that is, not only in terms of the constructive integration of signage into a building but also in terms of its relationship to a particular detail, material, or ground plan. Moreover, signage needs to relate to the utilization and history of the building, the site, and its surroundings. It is precisely when engaging with a difficult initial situation that integral thinking is required. In such cases the introduction of an unorthodox idea may not only help to solve a signage problem but also enable the designer to find a new form of expression. It is hoped that the strategies shown here will therefore provide inspiration for the discovery of other strategies, for this is a field that still offers enormous scope for experimentation.

The chapter "Signage Techniques" offers an overview of the most common signage methods. Historical techniques can be interpreted in contemporary ways and further developed. In principle, there are few limits to the ideas that can be explored, and digital technologies are offering extensive new scope for experimentation.

Finally, when discussing the topic of building signage, consideration also needs to be given to the influence on the quality of signage exercised by the different stakeholders involved: municipal authorities, building developers, manufacturers, graphic designers, architects, and construction managers. The questions that need to be considered here involve not only the concrete design and organization of projects and the provision of adequate budgets for these tasks but also the approach taken by stakeholders to signage commissions, their choice of contractors, and how they organize competitions. The book is rounded off by concrete, practical information on the fundamental planning processes required to design, manufacture, and mount building signage.

For a long time, the discussion of signage and lettering was shaped by a discourse focusing on what architecture "in itself" was able to communicate and what signage could contribute to its interpretation. This skewed relationship is now a thing of the past. It is only when architects and graphic designers enter into an open dialogue that the two disciplines are able mutually to enrich one another. Convincing, multilayered solutions are generated particularly when the theme of signage is integrated into the planning process at an early stage.

Part 1

INTRODUCTION

A BRIEF HISTORY OF ARCHIGRAPHY

History forms the humus that nourishes the creativity of designers and enables them to develop their disciplines. From a design-historical perspective, very few designs—whether architectural or graphic—are completely new inventions. Today, digital drafting and production techniques are providing additional support for a permanent process of variation and reinterpretation.

The current relevance of this theme warrants looking back at the historical development of this field. What discourses and design practices lie behind the styles of lettering on contemporary buildings? What are the basic motives and strategies that are shaping them?

Architectural ornament, ornament, lettering

In his essay "Ornament and Crime," written in 1908,[1] the Austrian architect Adolf Loos vilified building ornamentation as a superfluous element in modern architecture. This sentiment was indicative of a turn in architecture to the search for "pure" form, which resulted in a decrease in the perceived legitimacy of decorative elements as a means of structuring facades. Due to its informative and orienting function, lettering is in itself not an ornament but can become one through sequencing, repetition, and overlapping. Lettering reflects a certain economy: it can be deciphered by a literate population more quickly and unambiguously than older symbols and emblems. In 1995 the Swiss art historian Christoph Bignens[2] summarized the relationship between architectural form and lettering as follows: "Architectural form can at best connote the aim of a building whereas lettering on the building denotes it."[3] As a functional addition, lettering was spared the purification postulated and practiced by Loos and the representatives of the Neues Bauen (New Building) movement.

Neues Bauen architects derived design from the purpose it served, and in their view lettering accordingly needed to be matter-of-fact and modern, i.e., simple, structured, and free of decoration. However, from the 1910s to the 1930s, the styles of lettering created by Bauhaus designers and associated movements were not only plain and formally reduced like those by Herbert Bayer on the Bauhaus building itself in Dessau; this period also saw the creation of many experimental styles of lettering and advertising architectures that remain capable of surprising and thrilling today. The Bauhaus adopted ideas from, among others, Russian Constructivism. Representatives of the Dutch De Stijl movement and Italian Futurism also designed playfully utopian styles of lettering that extended to small, typographically tectonic, accessible structures and multimedia kiosks. Long before the evolution of Las Vegas, drawings were produced of buildings as a communication medium—facades covered with images, texts, and films. The Russians El Lissitzky and Gustavs Klucis, for instance, designed experimental speaker's platforms. Although most of these designs were abandoned before completion or not realized, they continue to contribute to debates about lettering and the mediatization of architecture.

From craft to design: new typography, new building

Whereas up until the beginning of the twentieth century, artisans, artists, sign painters, manufacturers, and architects had all designed and applied lettering, this situation began to change around the turn of the century due to an increased professionalization of the graphic arts. From the 1910s onward, the first applied arts schools with classes in graphic design were established in western Europe. Here, visual design and typography were taught systematically and from a modern perspective (left alignment, limited font selection, increased use of sans serif fonts, etc.).

The training provided at the Bauhaus, which was founded in 1919 in Weimar and moved to Dessau in 1925, proved to be seminal for both the graphic arts and architecture well into the postwar period.

The Bauhaus in Germany, as well as the lesser-known "Vchutemas" (Higher Art and Technical Studios) established in Moscow in 1920, experimented with combinations of handicraft and art. Those who taught at the Vchutemas included Wassily Kandinsky, who left Moscow in 1921 and later taught at the Bauhaus. A new element shared by both institutions was an explicitly interdisciplinary approach that brought together architects, graphic designers, and typographers under one roof and fundamentally influenced the emergence and development of the modern discipline of archigraphy. Designers used this approach to formulate modern concepts in the field of building signage, which at the time was still dominated by the use of classical Roman scripts and ornate lettering that was difficult to read.

Integration and composition

Inventions in the field of structural engineering at the end of the nineteenth and beginning of the twentieth century,

1 Walter Gropius and Adolf Meyer designed and built the Fagus factory in Alfeld an der Leine between 1911 and 1914. The two lines of lettering carefully positioned in the roof frieze were mounted in 1919.
2 + 3 Peter Behrens not only designed the AEG turbine factory in Berlin, which was completed in 1909, but also modernized the company logo.

4 The Bauhaus building in Dessau was built in 1928 by Walter Gropius and furnished with a sign by Herbert Bayer. The layout of the lettering on the facade became a new compositional element.
5 The Jelmoli department store in Zurich (1898) by Stadler and Usteri exhibits the gold and black, reverse painted bands of glass (fascias) typical of the time.

such as the steel skeleton structure, opened up new possibilities for architects. Curtain walls and large sections of closed wall required new design and technical strategies when it came to signage. The position on the facade, the orientation in relation to the building, and the choice of font—insofar as the latter was not predefined by a brand name or corporate design—became fields of compositional improvisation.

Industrialization produced new types of buildings such as factories, gas stations, exhibition halls, movie theaters, hotels, and, in the USA, motels. Avant-garde designers took on the task of producing signage for these new types of structures, and architects designed lettering specifically for particular buildings. Erich Mendelssohn developed customized illuminated lettering for department stores and entire light architectures. Factory buildings with meticulously integrated lettering by Peter Behrens and Walter Gropius became icons of architectural history. The brothers Hans and Wassili Luckhardt turned lettering on buildings into a new, defining, and advertising-oriented aspect of the facades of urban commercial buildings. Their run on designs—for instance, for the commercial building on Tauentzienplatz in Berlin, the front of which they remodeled into a facade devoted to advertising—earned them acclaim from advertising specialists but also criticism from colleagues who accused them of currying favor with the advertising industry. In their design for the Berlin-Haus on Potsdamer Platz they again endeavored to integrate lettering on the facade in a structurally appropriate manner.

International exchange in the interwar period

As a design center in the interwar period, the Bauhaus combined different currents, and as a consequence its methods and concepts of form gained international resonance. Along with influences from the young Soviet Union, it also took up many ideas from America—Ford's principles of rationalization, lifestyles associated with jazz, steel-frame constructions, and the architecture of Frank Lloyd Wright—that were already discussed at the Bauhaus in the 1920s in connection with the concept of "Americanism."

Due to the (forced) emigration of its protagonists in the 1930s, the design culture of the Bauhaus spread throughout the world. Following the closure of the Berlin Bauhaus in 1933, many "Bauhausers" immigrated to the USA, where they established successor institutions and taught at renowned art academies. In 1933 Black Mountain College was founded near Ashville in North Carolina. A number of leading Bauhaus figures taught there, including Walter Gropius. In 1937 the New Bauhaus was established in Chicago by *László Moholy-Nagy*. These schools provided training for many American architects and graphic designers who went on to achieve renown. Others—such as the graphic designer Paul Rand—were indirectly influenced by modernism.

In 1932 the exhibition *Modern Architecture: International Exhibition* at the *Museum of Modern Art* in New York and the accompanying book *The International Style* made modern architecture and its leading protagonists, including Walter Gropius and Ludwig Mies van der Rohe, well-known in the USA and stimulated a general interest in their work.

The mutual relationships and exchange of ideas in the period between the world wars led to a transatlantic homogenization of modern design in architecture and typography, even though the subsequent war was to rupture a number of these relationships, and Stalinism in the Soviet Union and National Socialism in Germany were to (temporarily) end the once-fruitful experimentation of the avant-garde.

Europe: the special case of England

While the ideas of Russian Constructivism and the Bauhaus attracted lively interest in many European countries (including Belgium, Czechoslovakia, and the Netherlands) and inspired prominent modernist building signage, for instance in Switzerland, in Britain the reaction was more restrained. Both architecture and typography there tended to remain oriented to classical traditions, as witnessed, for example, by the Arts and Crafts movement.

Until well into the twentieth century, the British cultivated a particular architectural lettering tradition. Letters were engraved directly into facades using, for the most part, classical fonts. Two typographers exercised a decisive influence in this respect, shaping English font creation at the beginning of the twentieth century and over subsequent decades: Edward Johnston and Eric Gill (who was also a sculptor). The principles they formulated were followed by many designers, such as the typographer and letter cutter Michael Harvey. In 1906 Johnston argued that the Roman Capitalis font and its variations were ideally suited to inscriptions because they were both easily legible and decorative.[4] He also contributed significantly to the precise coordination of lettering on facades.

In 1916 he designed the grotesque typeface[5] Johnston Sans, which was used throughout the London Underground

6 J. J. P. Oud built the Café de Unie in Rotterdam in 1925. The lettering and signage illumination are integrated into the facade, which shows the influence of the De Stijl and Constructivist movements.

7+8 Herbert Bayer's sketches of kiosks from 1924 are early examples of facades with integrated multimedia elements. Unfortunately never built, they were to have emitted smoke and sounds and shown films.

9 The 12-meter-high, diagonally extendible speaker's platform designed by El Lissitzky in 1924 was crowned by a screen intended for the display of slogans and the screening of films by night.

10 The speaker's platform by Gustav Klucis (1922) was part of a transportable "propaganda kiosk" equipped with features that included a screen and a bookstall.

11 In 1925 Alexander Rodchenko painted the slogan "Shoppers come/ to Mosselprom!" by Vladimir Mayakovsky on the six-story facade of the headquarters of the Moscow Rural Cooperative Administration, known by its abbreviation Mosselprom.

12 Maison de la Publicité, Oscar Nitzchke, Paris, 1936. The "media machine" was designed to project information generated inside it onto the Champs Elysées.

13 René Herbst installed his "luminographie" on the Pavillon de la Publicité in 1937. It was one of the main attractions at the International Expo held in Paris that year.

14 The Futurist Fortunato Depero in front of his pavilion for the publishing house Treves Tumminelli. The spectacular lettering sculpture was installed on the grounds of the Biennale held in Monza in 1927.

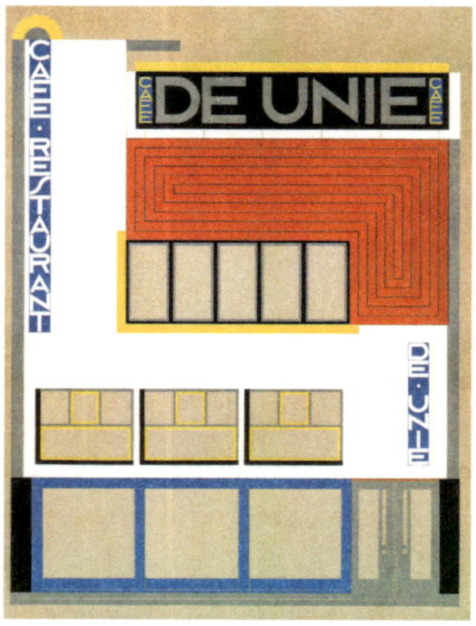

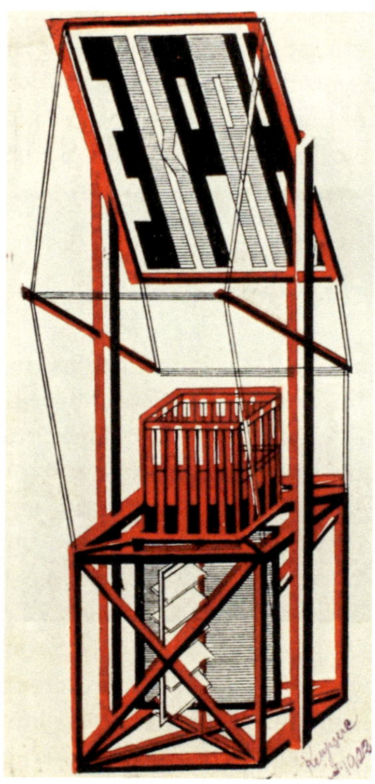

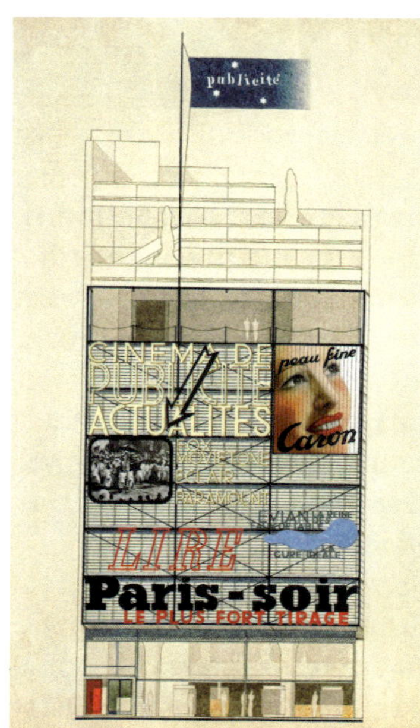

15 + 16 Stadtküche Kraft office building, Tauentzienstraße, Berlin, 1925. Hans and Wassili Luckhardt transformed old buildings into "modern" advertising facades, which attracted criticism from some quarters.
17 Erich Mendelssohn designed signage as an integral element of building facades. With the Schocken department store, built in Stuttgart in 1928, the lettering formed part of the lighting architecture.

18 One of several signage designs for the Berlin-Haus on Potsdamer Platz in Berlin, 1930. The Luckhardts explicitly endeavored to devise better ways of integrating advertising.
19 Apollo cinema, Zurich, 1928.

20 De Volharding, Den Haag, 1928. Jan Buijs was asked to design a facade with as much space as possible for advertising. The glass facade is interrupted by opaque strips with lettering on their interior surfaces. By night the building becomes an enormous light sculpture.
21 Ober department store, Zurich, 1934. The neon sign is heritage-protected.

system and consequently became widespread in British graphics, as did the Gill typeface designed by Eric Gill. However, the font that became most commonly used for archigraphics was English Vernacular, a more striking slab serif designed at the beginning of the nineteenth century for emerging advertising forms such as typographic posters, newspaper ads, and flyers.

More than any other nation, the British have cultivated a tradition of integral lettering forms that in graphic terms draw predominantly on classical models. This tradition has not only been cultivated in practice but has also been the subject of numerous publications: books on the subject by Nicolete Gray,[6] Jock Kinneir,[7] Allan Bartram,[8] and Phil Baines and Catherine Dixon[9] present an inspiring array of building lettering. It was Nicolete Gray who established the Central Lettering Record (CLR) at St. Martins College, a database for which she collected thousands of images. Today the collection is supervised by Catherine Dixon and Phil Baines.[10]

The lettering experiments of the avant-garde are referred to by most British authors—if at all—only in passing. While at the end of her book Gray addresses a number of modern examples, for instance from the Netherlands, Alan Bartram limits himself to what he sees as the "only relevant" English and Italian forms of lettering. Jock Kinneir also bypasses European modernism, writing in 1980 (!) that the waves following Art Nouveau never found broad acceptance. He characterizes De Stjil as formalistic and intellectual, and Art Deco as insignificant. However, he does regard a number of Swiss and German examples from the postwar period as having found acceptance—styles that, although strongly oriented to the reduced typography of modernism, employed newly developed fonts (Helvetica, Univers, etc.).

England is an exemplary case of the divergent attitudes of the great cultural-historical movements finding expression. Humanist-informed design approaches were followed by technical-rational approaches and vice versa. No one approach was able to completely displace the other, and both coexisted in the fields of architecture and design independently of what was publicly perceived as the dominant direction at any one time.

In an essay published in 2007, the English designer and journalist Jock Kinneir looks back at the situation in Great Britain:

> "Britain was late to modernism in the twentieth century. (…) In the architecture and design of 1945 and after, the British way was various and tempered."[11]

"Modernism," as used here by Kinneir, refers to the postwar period, during which the avant-garde concepts of the interwar period in both architecture and graphic design—refined and above all condensed—had reached their high point. One of the few Englishmen interested in the European avant-garde was the young graphic designer and journalist Herbert Spencer, who traveled through Europe in the 1930s and 1940s. There he met Piet Zwart and Max Bill and became acquainted with their design principles. Spencer subsequently disseminated their typographic innovations in the journal *Typografica*, which he edited from 1949 until 1967, thereby influencing a number of young English designers and typographers, who drew on these styles in their designs of building lettering. Edward Wright's multilingual, colorful signage on the pavilion for the 6th International Union of Architects (UIA) Congress, which took place in London in 1961, represents a rare but successful example.

The "Swiss Style" and lettering

The "Swiss Style"[12] was founded by a group of designers that included Theo Ballmer, Max Bill, and Xanti Schawinky, who began to work in Switzerland after completing their training at the Bauhaus. Their aim was to take Swiss graphic design to a higher and above all international level. They achieved this through extensive publication on the subject in journals such as *Graphis*, *Spirale*, *Neue Grafik*, and *Typografische Monatsblätter*, exhibitions, and lecture programs. Representatives of the Zurich school, in particular Josef Müller-Brockmann, and of the Basel school, such as Armin Hofmann, were invited to the USA and later to Japan and other countries.

Typographers and graphic designers from German-speaking Switzerland interested in constructive design were inspired above all by Anton Stankowski, Jan Tschichold, Paul Schuitema, and Piet Zwart. In the 1950s "Swiss typography" was recognized as a "rational typographic style." Many designers who were trained and worked in Switzerland went on to work in France, Italy, the USA, and other countries and in the process took Swiss graphic design and typography out into the world.

Clear typography for effective wayfinding

The font designs by the Swiss designers Adrian Frutiger and Max Miedinger, with their emphasis on easy legibility,

22 Sketches by Arne Jacobsen for prominent signage on the Stelling Hus in Copenhagen.
23 Max Bill's gigantic lettering designed to be integrated into the window apertures of the Corso building.
24 In the variation that was implemented, neon letters dance in a high arch above the variety theater, Zurich, 1934.

25 The Stelling Hus built in 1935 with small lettering above the entrance.
26 Ernst Gaberel's design for a lettering frieze around a company headquarters in Davos, circa 1930. Lettering played an important role in many of Gaberel's projects.

27 Monumental facade painting by Ernst Keller for a paper company in Zurich, circa 1930.
28 Modern lettering composition by Max Bill on the Zett-Haus in Zurich, 1932.

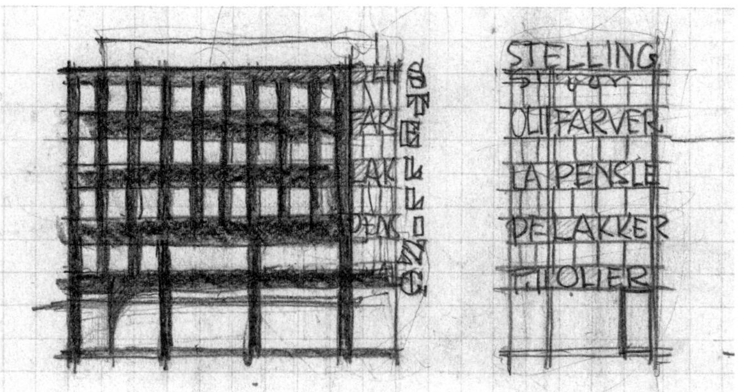

29 False front with neon sign on the Urban cinema in Zurich, 1934.
30 By day the problematic relationship between the giant supporting frame and the small, two-story building is conspicuous.

31 When illuminated, the eight-meter-high, red neon letters P, S, F, S (Philadelphia Savings Bank) can be seen from as far as 32 kilometers away. George Howe and William Lescaze built this high-rise in 1932.
32 In 1934, Jan Duiker installed a giant sign on the roof of the Cinéac cinema in Amsterdam and a second sign at right angles to the facade.

33 + 34 Jelmoli department store extension designed by Otto Pfleghard, Zurich, 1938. An "advertising niche" on the sixth floor featured 2.6-meter-high letters mounted on four horizontal poles.
35 In 1930 light beams shone through a stencil projected an image of the Persil brand name measuring 750 x 400 meters onto cloud cover.

proved popular particularly in the field of orientation design—today known as signaletics [Signaletics, p. 36 ff]—from the 1960s to the 1980s. Adrian Frutiger immigrated to Paris in the 1950s to work as a font designer. In 1957 he published the Univers font; at the same time, Max Meidinger brought Helvetica onto the market, which remains the most frequently used font for signage. These clinical, neutral, and modern grotesque fonts also proved particularly well suited to the architecture of postwar modernism.

The Swiss designer and teacher Josef Müller-Brockmann and other leading design figures developed new design parameters for the use of fonts in layouts. The grid-like arrangement of texts and symbols in the print space of books was adopted for signaletics and allowed information in one or more languages to be structured in signage systems on different scale levels and in different formats.

With their aspiration to universality, strict signaletic systems represent a clear contrast to the context-specific facade signage denoted by archigraphy. For this reason, only a few examples of integral building lettering emerged during the heyday of classic signaletics. During the 1950s and 1960s, the Italian architect and designer Carlo Scarpa designed handsome, architecturally specific lettering, and a number of almost pop-style examples of building lettering from the late 1960s, with their playful and expressive forms, point to the coming epoch.

The end of the International Style

Towards the end of the 1960s, criticism grew of the rigid formalism of commercial architecture. The great age of the functionalist "International Style" came to an end,[13] and the field of graphic design underwent far-reaching changes. In postwar modernism the culture of lettering had declined in importance. Standardized brand and corporate design elements replaced individual, customized signage. Office blocks with grid facades or large windows offered hardly any space for lettering. Office suburbs with standardized rentable areas emerged that facilitated rapid changes in use by avoiding the assertion of a clear identity. The unity of interior structure and exterior form postulated by classical modernism gave way to an abstract facade architecture onto which logos could be applied and rapidly replaced with others where required.

Let's play

An important ideational and formal basis for the subsequent changes in architecture and graphic design was the pop art movement, which emerged independently in the USA and England in the 1950s. Its protagonists focused on the trivial and everyday (for example, Claes Oldenburg with his sculptures of absurdly enlarged everyday objects), aestheticized trademarks (Andy Warhol with his legendary screen prints), exaggerated elements of popular culture (Roy Lichtenstein's images based on comics), and excessive mass consumption.

This shrill and striking representation of the ordinary directly influenced the experiments of early postmodern architects and designers in California. In 1965, American landscape architect and graphic artist Barbara Stauffacher Solomon's colorfully expressive designs for the interiors of the Sea Ranch resort in California by architect Charles Moore made her one of the most important representatives of the supergraphics movement. The term was coined by architectural critic C. Ray Smith, who regarded supergraphics not as a "decorative tool but rather spatial experimentation."[14] The North American big signs of the 1960s and 1970s reshaped entire buildings with abstract symbols and created a new type of lettering. The designer Deborah Sussman began to work with postmodern architects such as Frank Gehry and in 1984 developed a bright, colorful look for the Olympic Games in Los Angeles. In the parallel theorization of the concept of "postmodern" by the US architectural critic Charles Jencks and the architects Denise Scott Brown, Robert Venturi, and Steven Izenour, a decisive role was played by sign systems and their expressive and large-scale use on buildings.

Learning from Las Vegas

The two books *Complexity and Contradiction in Architecture* (1966)[15] and *Learning from Las Vegas* (1972)[16] gave rise to an important and overdue debate in the field of architectural theory. It centered on the question of the increasing loss in the postwar period of architecture's symbolic content and the value of graphic symbols. Modernism's attempt to rationalize the foundations of design, it was argued, had failed. Modernist architects had also drawn on historical models and—for example in the industrial aesthetic—recast them in a manner specific to their time. The attempt to define architecture in purely spatial-functional

36 The gilded "U" mounted on the Union brewery is one of Dortmund's major landmarks. In 2010 an LED frieze was installed on the top story of the building, which today is used as a cultural center.
37 Expressive "letter spheres" by Gérard Miedinger on the Bally building – headquarters of the architecture firm of Häfeli, Moser Steiger in Zurich,1968.

38 The illustrative wall design for the Bally building on Bleicherweg in Zurich was produced by Josef Müller-Brockmann (1955).
39 The free lettering composition by Max Bill on the Pestalozzi building in Zurich dating from 1943 is witness to the designer's interest lettering in combination with architecture and the diversity of his work in this field of design.
40 The Studio 4 cinema in Zurich was remodeled and furnished with stylish signage by Roman Clemens in 1948/49.

41 Handsome, integrated relief lettering designed by Carlo Scarpa in 1957 for the Olivetti shop in Venice.

42 + 43 The ultimate "decorated shed": The faceless mail order firm in the Philadelphia agglomeration is identified solely by the 10-meter-high, bright red lettering spelling out BASCO. Venturi, Scott Brown Ass. (VSBA), 1976.
44 This roasted poultry outlet in Flanders/NY became the icon of a debate. VSBA used the term "duck" to refer to a building that as a whole constituted a single symbol.

45 Carefully integrated lettering on Guild House by VSBA, Philadelphia, 1964.

46 The "Indeterminate Facade" designed by SITE for the BEST department store chain in Houston, 1974.
47 The "Peeling Facade" by SITE in Richmond dating from 1974: Humorous corporate architecture "avant la lettre" for the BEST department store.
48 The Lieb House by VSBA, New Jersey, 1969.
49 Las Vegas welcome sign in the Googie style, Las Vegas, 1959.

terms had failed and had never corresponded to the built reality of its most important representatives, including Le Corbusier, Walter Gropius, and Ludwig Mies van der Rohe.

Denise Scott Brown, Robert Venturi, and Steven Izenour antagonized Neues Bauen adherents with their call for the active and playful (re)integration of ornamentation, lettering, and advertising motifs into architectural designs, and mounted a front assault against functionalist modernism. Their ideas triggered what was in some cases massive resistance from architectural colleagues, teaching institutions, cultural historians, and journalists.

The refinement of the ordinary

The projects undertaken by the firm of Venturi, Scott Brown and Associates (VSBA) from 1963 onward were a provocation for its contemporaries (as were Wolfang Weingart's graphic designs a bit later for the Swiss design community). Although the "decorated shed"—an architecturally inexpressive "box" made of corrugated metal and identified by large-scale lettering, for example as a distribution center within an urban agglomeration—constitutes a topos of their work, other projects reveal a more differentiated approach to graphic design and architecture. In the case of Guild House, built in Philadelphia in 1963, the carefully positioned lettering is part of a complex symbolic system that aims ironically but also affectionately to give an identity to the inhabitants of this rest home. In a similar manner, the large lettering on Fire Station No. 4 in Columbus, Indiana (1966), coalesces with architectural elements in order to indicate the significance of the building as a part of the public infrastructure. Irony and striking and unsettling effects are thus certainly strategies characteristic of the work of VSBA. However, they also provided important points of departure for new architectural and graphic compositions. Around the same time, the New York architectural firm SITE attracted attention with its ironic use of lettering on buildings. In the 1970s and 1980s, its designs for the department store chain BEST set standards in a field that today is referred to as "corporate architecture". These architects also experimented with large-scale, ornamentally used lettering [BEST-Anti-Sign Building, p. 128].

Reception and aesthetic refinement

The theories of VSBA had an impact throughout the world and led to exhibitions in the USA, Asia, and Europe. In 1979, for example, the Swiss art historian Stanislaus von Moos mounted an exhibition in Zurich's Museum für Gestaltung (Museum of Design). Both the exhibition and the publications associated with it exerted an influence on the generation of Swiss architects working at the time and their successors. Both Mike Guyer of Gigon/Guyer and Daniel Niggli of EM2N have confirmed this in interviews with the authors. In their Davos projects Gigon/Guyer also drew on the historical, modernistic building signage of the architect Rudolf Gaberel.

In the 1980s few European architects drew inspiration so willingly and directly from the USA as the Frenchman Jean Nouvel, who was one of the first in his field to design media facades and lettering systems. He also wrote on this theme, arguing that lettering and new media needed to be integrated while also being tamed and transcended.[17]

At the same time, the Swiss architects Jacques Herzog and Pierre de Meuron began to integrate lettering into their designs, although in a more restrained fashion than Nouvel. They worked predominantly in the physical-material field, while also designing media facades and buildings furnished with LED strips, which, however, remained unrealized.

One of their first lettering projects was a garden pavilion in the form of a poetic lettering sculpture [E,D,E,N, 1987, p. 62]. Whereas Nouvel used large-format screen printing on glass to create striking effects in spite of its transparency, in the case of the SUVA building in Basel, Herzog & de Meuron utilized this technique in the form of a small-scale lettering ornament which is semitransparent, thereby simultaneously veiling and offering a view of the historical facade. The building's self-identification takes the form of thousands of silk-screened letters only a few centimeters high, reflecting Herzog & de Meuron's general avoidance of large-scale lettering.

The Basel-based architects also developed various new techniques with which images and ornaments can be integrated into facades. They worked closely with the Swiss artist Rémy Zaugg over several decades to create poetic and in some cases provocative (illuminated) signage on their buildings.

The Swiss architectural firm of Gigon/Guyer attracted attention at the beginning of the 1990s with several designs for the typographical formulation of which they enlisted the

50 Supergraphic by Jean-Philippe Lenclos, Ecole Les Maradas, Cergy Pontoise, 1972.
51 BEST "Anti-Sign Building," SITE, Richmond, 1978.
52 Wall design by Edward Wright, 6th World Congress of Architecture, London, 1961.
53 Deborah Sussmann: colorful signage on a Joseph Magnin store by Frank Gehry, 1969.

54 Flagship project of postmodernism: the Niban-Kan building in Tokyo by Minoru Takeyama, 1977. "All over" facade design by Jean-Philippe Lenclos.
55 + 58 Section of the monumental facade graphic by Jean Philippe-Lenclos. Gandolys-Werft, Port Barcarès, 1969.

56 Restrained, single-color signage by Barbara Stauffacher-Solomon on the wooden facade of the Sea Ranch visitor center designed by Charles Moore, Sonoma/CA, 1976.
57 Colorful interior graphics: Stauffacher-Solomon's congenial graphic statements inside the building.

59 Aldo Rossi, Centro Torri, shopping center in Parma, 1988. The towers, the brickwork and the ceramic signage refer to the local building culture.

60 Design for a theater in Blois, Herzog und de Meuron, 1991. Facade with LED ticker displays (not constructed).

61 Jean Nouvel and Gilbert Lézénès: cheerful "billboard" on the La Coupole cultural center in Combs la Ville, 1987.

62 Jean Nouvel and Emmanuel Cattani, Cartier, Villars-sur-Glâne, 1992. The logo as ornament, integrated here in the reflective facade, creating artful effects with the changing incidence of light.

63 Semiotic veil: thousands of logos screen-printed onto a glass facade. SUVA building, Herzog and de Meuron, Basel, 1993.

64 The lettering changes the dimensions of the building: Coop retail group HQ, Zurich, 1999.

65 E, D, E, N, pavilion by Herzog and De Meuron, Rheinfelden, 1987 [see page 62].

help of designer Lars Müller and graphic artist Trix Wetter.[18] From 1996 onward the Munich-based architects Hild und K made their own distinctive contribution to the lettering and newly kindled ornamentation debate [Sammeln, p. 25; Hotel Louis, p. 68].

Signaletics combined with visual narration

In the mid-1990s, the French-Swiss graphic designer Ruedi Baur began questioning the functional premises of the first generation of signaletics designers. While he was also influenced by pop art and postmodernism, his main focus was on the sociopolitical aspects of communication in public space. Baur had learned his craft in the early 1980s with the Swiss signaletics designer Theo Ballmer. He came away from this experience convinced that signaletics as it was conventionally practiced was rigid and devoid of creativity,[19] and as a result it was many years before he once again became interested in the field.

Baur's large-scale facade design for the École Supérieure d'Ingénieurs Spécialisés en Systèmes Automatiques et Robotiques (ESISAR) in Valence (1998) and subsequent projects brought new ideas to the field of signaletics. Today he sees his playful designs as a deliberate move away from rational and supposedly objective Swiss functionalism taught at art academies and practiced well into the 1980s. In Baur's view, every building requires a context-specific, individual solution. He has established international networks, working intensively with architects and product and font designers. His designs have gone far beyond the objective of providing information and are more narrative than classic signaletics systems. He has often referenced the history of the building or the neighborhood in his projects and worked again directly onto and with the facades. Even though in some of Baur's projects the lettering layer seems almost too ebullient, he has set international standards and opened up this field for the current third generation of building signage and signaletics designers.

Lettering culture in the 21st century

Since the end of the 1990s, designers throughout the world have increasingly produced syntheses between building lettering and elements of signaletics. Today, a number of lettering and signaletics designers are again pursuing more hands-on strategies, creating integral lettering designs that draw on the qualities of the architecture concerned, its context, and its history. A new aspect can be seen in the fact that signaletics designers are also increasingly endeavoring to derive wayfinding elements and lettering for building interiors from the external signage, or at least to coordinate their designs with the architecture in terms of materials and colors.

Since the turn of the millennium, a clearly perceptible international dynamic has been shaping the lettering sector. Swiss design firms such as Bringolf Irion Vögeli GmbH (Zurich) and Hi – Visuelle Kommunikation (Lucerne), German design agencies including L2M3 (Stuttgart) and büro uebele (Stuttgart), and the Viennese designer Erwin K. Bauer have introduced new impulses. Interesting projects have also been realized in the Benelux countries, eastern Europe, Scandinavia, the USA (Pentagram design agency), and Australia.

More recently established architectural firms such as Christ & Gantenbein (Basel) and EM2N (Zurich) are involving graphic and signaletics designers in early project phases and consulting with typographers. Furthermore, there are a growing number of graphic designers who are well acquainted with spatial concepts and capable of analyzing and interpreting architectures. In the future—it is to be hoped—reservations about collaboration between the two disciplines will increasingly disappear.

1 Adolf Loos, "Ornament und Verbrechen" (1908), in Adolf Loos, *Sämtliche Schriften* (Vienna: Herold, 1962).
2 *Archithese* 1 (Schrift am Bau. Calligrafie et facade) (1995): 1.
3 Ibid.
4 Edward Johnston, *Writing—Illuminating—Lettering* (London: John Hog, 1906).
5 Grotesque fonts are sans serif designs.
6 Nicolete Gray, *Lettering on Buildings* (London: Architectural Press, 1960).
7 Jock Kinneir, *Words on Buildings: The Art and Practice of Public Lettering* (London: Architectural Press, 1980).
8 Alan Bartram, *Lettering in Architecture* (London: Lund Humphries, 1975).
9 Phil Baines and Catherine Dixon, *Signs: Lettering the Environment* (London: Laurence King, 2003).
10 http://www.publiclettering.org.uk/
11 Jock Kinneir, *Signs at the Royal Festival Hall* (London: Hyphen Press, 2007).
12 The emergence of the term "Swiss Style" and its international dissemination is described in detail by Christoph Bignens in his book *Swiss Style – die grosse Zeit der Schweizer Gebrauchsgrafik 1914–1964* (Zurich: Chronos, 2000).
13 Bignens concludes: "In general terms the belief in a normative aesthetic that could once and for all define a high standard for the fine as well as applied arts disappeared in the 1960s." See Bignens, *Swiss Style*.
14 Tony Brook and Adrian Shaughnessy, *Supergraphics Transforming Space: Graphic Design for Walls, Buildings & Spaces* (London: Unit Editions), 258.
15 Robert Venturi, *Complexity and Contradiction in Architecture* (New York: Museum of Modern Art Press, 1966).
16 Venturi/Scott Brown/Izenour, *Learning from Las Vegas* (Cambridge, MA: MIT Press, 1972).
17 Olivier Boissière, *Jean Nouvel, Emmanuel Cattani und Partner* (Zurich: Artemis Verlag, 1992).
18 Authors' interview with Mike Guyer of May 4, 2015.
19 Authors' interview with Ruedi Baur of March 31, 2015.

66 Vinikus restaurant, Davos, designed by Gigon and Guyer and featuring optimally integrated lettering using a discreet color variation designed by Lars Müller, 1992.
67 HinderSchlatterFeuz designed the lettering on the Noerd office building using standard neon tubes, Zurich, 2009.
68 Stephan Rutz's fluorescent-tube lettering on the F + F School for Art and Media Design in Zurich, 2004.

69 Since 1994 the facade of the Vinikus shop and restaurant has been painted bright red.

70 Christoph T. Hunziker's construction art design on the fire brigade building in Winterthur luminesces, 1999.
71 Extremely reduced lettering by Mayo Bucher on the Emmen shopping center, Emmenbrücke, 2000.
72 Between legibility and abstraction: car shelter/maintenance depot at the Zurich civil engineering authority (TAZ)—Laube, Kaufmann and Widrig, Zurich, 2004.

73 Large welcoming gesture: Lehigh Valley Hospital by VSBA, Muhlenberg/USA, 2005.
74 The Minnaert university building by Neutelings Riedjik Architects stands on a lettering plinth, Utrecht, 1997.
75 Gilded prefabricated concrete elements: recycling station by Hild und K in Landshut, 1996.
76 Lettering sculpture with 1980s flair at the former Fiat factory in Turin (Lingotto), 1988.
77 Gigantism in the new millennium. The lettering on the Bosch car park near Stuttgart is 8 meters high and accessible from the interior.
78 The letters, which were manufactured by the Westiform firm, are covered with tensioned fabric.

79 Realities:united developed this media facade together with the Singapore firm WOHA in 2009: a high-resolution LED screen in the midst of 500 colored LED elements that extend its effect.
80 A pixel matrix made up of 1800 lighting elements: art as part of an marketing campaign for untenanted office space, Potsdamer Platz, Berlin, 2005 (realities:united).

81 The old "Ku'damm-Eck" (Ku'damm Corner) in Berlin was designed by Werner Düttmann between 1969 and 1972 and featured a 300-square-meter light-grid advertising panel that could display colored and moving images.
82 Sketch by VSBA for a gigantic screen with 200,000 "electronically programmed lights," College Football Hall of Fame, New Jersey, 1967.
83 Unrealized, flag-like "electronic billboard" at the Whitehall Ferry Terminal in New York, VSBA, 1995.

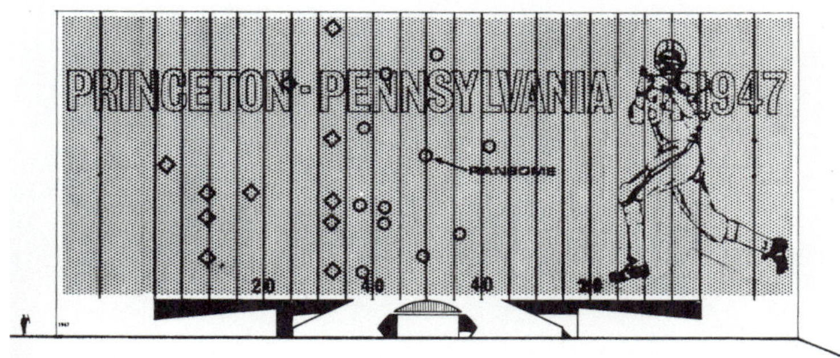

SELF- AND THIRD-PARTY ADVERTISING

THE CASE FOR A DIFFERENTIATED APPROACH

Information and advertisements on buildings are not an isolated aesthetic or economic phenomenon. While the focus of this publication is on facades—the locus where signage, advertisements, and wayfinding elements meet with architecture—these layers of symbols at the same time constitute a complex communicative system in urban space. They communicate different contents and values to the beholder.[1] What distinguishes building signage from (exterior) advertising? What is meant by self-advertising and third-party advertising? The following is an attempt to define and reevaluate these concepts.

Self-advertising, third-party advertising, wayfinding

Lettering, symbols, and images attached to buildings inform, advertise, and provide orientation. Different terms—at least in the German-speaking world—are used for these three categories: self-advertising *(Eigenwerbung)*, third-party advertising *(Fremdwerbung)*, and wayfinding *(Wegleitung)* or signaletics. These terms refer to the meaning of symbols in relation to architecture: do they have a thematic relationship with it, do they direct the attention of the beholder away from it, or do they support its orienting function?

Self-advertising: Contains what it says on the label

Architecture-specific building signage, for which the term *archigraphy* is proposed here, relates specifically to the building to which it is affixed. Such signage thus has a direct thematic connection with the building concerned; it identifies the building and helps with orientation in the urban space by making the sought-after location recognizable. As a result, it is less often called into question—where its execution is not too dominant—than commercial advertising. It also lends itself to better integration in the architecture, particularly in cases where structures are designed for long-term or unchanging use. Archigraphics strengthen the identity of buildings and locations and can thus contribute to the definition of urban locations. For this reason archigraphics are an integral part of territorially anchored architecture and should support it in terms of what they express.

Conflicts between corporate design and architecture

Corporate identities are seldom developed with reference to their spatial effect and utilization. Today branding concepts are applied across different media and must function on diverse platforms. Exterior signage is an important business card for every enterprise but is in most cases dealt with only marginally in the development of corporate designs. As a result, company logos—particularly when they contain complex symbols—do not usually allow for effective structural integration on facades. Word marks—especially when they are composed of capital letters—are considerably better suited to this purpose. Another possibility is the standardization of different letterings and logos in terms of material and color, for example in upmarket shopping arcades. In the Galleria Milano, for instance, all the lettering is in gold on black glass, and in Rail-City in Zurich's main railway station, all lettering is in black on white strips. This is not really satisfactory, however, because brands, which often change, are diametrically opposed to territorially anchored architecture.

Firms that invest in carefully designed architecture as an expression of their corporate culture (corporate architecture) are increasingly realizing that investment in logos designed only for the short term makes little financial sense and are therefore becoming open to the idea of architecturally specific signage [Raiffeisen, p. 64]. A recent tendency in graphic design has also seen designers deriving lettering from the characteristics of the architecture concerned and using it in both their signage and their corporate design.

Promotion becomes (third-party) advertising

After 1930 the German term *Reklame* (promotion)[2] was increasingly replaced by *Werbung* (advertising).[3] With advertising, companies endeavor to draw attention to their products, brands, and services and to encourage consumers to buy. In spite of this, the outmoded term *Reklame* is still used today for noncommercial signage. This is confusing. Architecture-specific building signage and self- and third-party advertising should be more decisively distinguished from each other and based on separate legal foundations, approval procedures, and guidelines.

Against the "advertising deluge"

Since they have existed on a larger scale, trademarks, advertising, and company logos on facades have tended to polarize opinion. However, the discourse has predominantly involved experts: urban planners, architects, cultural heritage associations, monument conservators, and advertisers.

The German printing firm owner and publisher Ernst Litfass developed the so-called *Litfasssäule*—a pillar displaying advertising—in reaction to early criticism of advertising displays. In 1855, after a long period of negotiation with the municipality of Berlin, he was permitted to erect hundreds of these advertising and information pillars. It was an attempt to contain or remove the deluge of posters plastered on facades, firewalls, balustrades, and handrails and, by restricting them to a specifically designed structure, to integrate them into the cityscape.

Today most municipalities have postering contracts with the advertising industry that regulate the placement of posters and placards in urban space—their dimensions, distribution, and density. The degree to which the graphic quality of advertising posters has changed is rarely discussed. The focus is on the "appropriate" integration of advertising vehicles in urban space, and this is a malleable concept.

Around 1900 the economist and social policy minister Viktor Mataja vividly described the general state of exterior advertising in the city of Vienna:[4]

> Public touting as a means of publicity is today stifled by street noise and, as a result, has significantly decreased in importance. The distribution of what are as a rule meagerly designed notifications (dodgers, handbills) has also become outmoded. [...] Instead, advertisements on walls and boards of all kinds have become extraordinarily widespread in both appropriate and inappropriate locations. They follow us from lanes into tram carriages, the railway station, and other public places. And we do not escape these advertisements, which speak to us in words and images, when we leave the city. Panels escort us along the railway tracks,[5] and the familiar sign greets us on rocks and buildings in places unfamiliar to us.

At the beginning of the twentieth century, cultural heritage associations were founded in many places and for decades sought vigorously to counter the "disfigurement of cities with advertising":[6]

> Since their beginnings the efforts of cultural heritage associations have been directed against the advertising that forces itself into the foreground with its noisy ostentation in places where the eye seeks calm and rest. [...] Does it not cling unexpectedly to windows, facades, firewalls, and balconies, clamber like an ape onto the cornices, even onto the roofs?

Over the course of the following decades, the arguments of the opponents of advertising changed. Whereas at the beginning of the twentieth century the focus was still on the protection of the "intact landscape of the homeland" and the buildings in historic town centers, *Neues Bauen* architects criticized advertising for tarnishing the modern cityscape. As the mobility of populations increased, traffic safety became a major concern. Traffic signs needed to be clearly visible. Following the Second World War, criticism was directed at the economic absurdity of the "orderless mass of advertisements" which left many different logos competing with one another on facades. In 1965, the Highway Beautification Act was passed in the USA in an attempt to limit exterior advertising along arterial roads and highways. In many places, the resistance of opponents of advertising led to the introduction of statutory regulations, municipal guidelines, and a unified approval procedure.

Third-party advertising and architecture

From the perspective of architecture, commercial advertising is a foreign body, since it forms no thematic relationship to the building to which it is attached and accordingly cannot and should not be integrated into it. The trademarks and names of firms and services offered by nonlocal or global providers direct attention away from the architecture. If they become dominant and spread out over the architecture, they degrade it into a pure advertising vehicle. Moreover, if the same logos appear worldwide, cityscapes become interchangeable. Commercial advertising thus contributes to a weakening of specific, local urban identities. A distinction needs to be made here in terms of how advertising is structured across cities. Making space available for large-scale advertising in specific recreational areas—such as Times Square, Piccadilly Circus, St. Pauli in Hamburg, etc.—is better suited to preserving the overall character of a cityscape than limiting the size of advertising and in return allowing its distribution over a wider area.

84 Posts and signage panels are clearly visible in William Hogarth's painting from 1755.
85 Ads everywhere! The scene at Zurich railroad station around 1910 is typical of its time.
86 Following the restoration of the Galleria in Milan in 2014–15, all the logos are once again in gold on black, as they were when the building was first opened in 1867.
87 Are graphically unified logos only possible when artists work alongside architects? Mayo Bucher, Shoppi Tivoli, Spreitenbach, 2014.

88 The famous poster pillar developed by Ernst Litfass brought a degree of order from 1855 onward.
89 1932: During the "Lighting Week" in Zurich, the new medium was explored in diverse ways.

90 From a contemporary perspective, fascinating, diverse, and colorful: illuminated advertising on Europahaus in Berlin in the 1930s.
91 Participants in Zurich's "Lighting Week" in 1932 included renowned designers such as Max Bill and Hans Finsler.

Exterior advertising is visible to all

From the perspective of the advertising industry, architecture—along with public space—is an ideal advertising medium. Here messages are visible to everybody. At a time when markets are becoming highly fragmented and groups targeted via TV and the Internet—where advertising can be switched off or blocked—are increasingly difficult to reach, exterior advertising[7] is once again becoming an important medium. For architecture, this is having consequences whose effects will only increase in the future as a result of new, digital advertising forms involving (interactive) screens with moving pictures.

Building signage and architecture

The physical appearance of the city is primarily shaped by building volumes, interim spaces, thoroughfare networks, and squares. However, since industrialization, the "speaking" layers of symbols that lie over and between architecture have multiplied and thereby fundamentally changed communication in urban spaces.

Building signage shapes the optical effect of architecture; it defines buildings, in some cases places them in competition with one another, and explicitly communicates. It is inseparably connected with the development of modern architecture and the disciple of urban planning. In the past, this led architects to complain about the loss of sole responsibility in terms of the expression, interpretation, and legibility of their works. Their status as universalists changed fundamentally in the twentieth century, which was marked by mechanization, rationalization, and above all an increasing division of labor. In the meantime, they have become accustomed to integrating a range of planning specialists—including signaletics specialists, typographers, and designers—into their work processes. Such specialists are often faced with the problem of devising signage and lettering for buildings whose architecture is determined by the need for the highest possible degree of usage flexibility, which in turn prevents the assertion of a clear identity. However, depending on the building type, different, context-specific strategies can be applied to overcome such problems [case studies from p. 42].

Third-party advertising in public space

While at the pedestrian level advertising does not present a problem, when it is located on the upper sections of buildings it exerts an effect on the entire building volume. In this context, conflicts emerge in terms of effective aesthetics that remain unresolved today. Problems develop in particular when different logos are juxtaposed on facades and, as a result, cannibalize one another. Whereas on the one hand it is agreed that advertising belongs in a lively, contemporary cityscape, on the other its legitimacy is today again being increasingly questioned. In a number of countries and cities (São Paulo,[8] Bergen, Grenoble, and a number of states in the USA) third-party advertising has even been completely banned. These debranding strategies fundamentally question the commercialization of architecture (and public space) by private enterprise. In the advertising industry such ideas naturally meet with opposition, while urban populations tend to be ambivalent on the subject. According to surveys conducted in São Paulo, the population has reacted positively to the dismantling of advertising facilities. However, city inhabitants also want to be informed about the latest products, brands, and services. They are addressed as consumers and as such are part of marketing strategies. However, it seems that they are also becoming accustomed to new forms of advertising and are learning to some extent to block them out. Moreover, advertising forms that were once considered disturbing—such as billboards and product posters—are today becoming sought-after collector's items. Early commercial murals and historical illuminated signs are being placed under preservation orders and included in museum collections.

Regulation

The task of city authorities is to regulate the different actors and claims falling within their jurisdictions. However, most municipalities exhibit a certain degree of ambivalence in the way they approach advertising. On the one hand, they pass laws and produce differentiated concepts that ensure quality (through the appropriate integration of advertising in architecture and urban space) and that—when a clear distinction is made between building signage and exterior advertising—contribute to a productive signage culture. On the other hand, for over a century they have participated in the increasing commercialization of cities by renting out public space to private firms. Such space cannot be increased and is an important asset. When it is rented out to private enterprise for commercial purposes, the question arises as to whether the municipalities—and thereby the public—are adequately profiting from such arrangements. Beyond making design recommendations, municipalities could contractually oblige the advertising industry to make its earnings public and set fees for the rental of advertising space accordingly. Moreover, it could be stipulated that the authorities must provide city inhabitants with information concerning how the income from such agreements is being spent.

Promoting signage culture

For the reasons outlined above, it makes sense to produce specific guidelines relating to signage and its coordination with architecture. Such guidelines can relate to not only constructive integration but also visual, material, social, and historical contextualization. Municipalities should ensure that the relevant legal foundations and approval procedures are adapted to such signage. In addition, signage culture could be given targeted promotion by means of financial incentives (for example, the waiving of fees), the organization of competitions, and the awarding of prizes.

1 Apart from legal forms of expression approved and regulated by legislators and municipalities, there also exist many illegal playful, political, and artistic layers of symbols.
2 French *réclame*, literally "calling into memory": *réclamer*; Latin *reclamare*, "call loudly, shout."
3 *Propaganda*, on the other hand, refers to political advertising.
4 Victor Mataja, *Die Reklame* (Berlin/Leipzig: Duncker und Humboldt, 1909/1920).
5 So-called *Streckenwerbung* (route advertising).
6 H. Balsiger, "Plakat oder Reklameunfug?" *Heimatschutz = Patrimoine 7* (1922): 119–22.
7 Today often referred to as Out-of-home-Media (OohM).
8 In 2007 Mayor Gilberto Kassab brought the Lei Cidade Limpa ("Clean City Law") into force.

SIGNALETICS

In principle, a distinction can be made between normative, that is, legally regulated, signalization forms—such as those relating to street, rail, and air traffic—and facultative signaletics systems, which are for the most part oriented to nonmotorized traffic, although today the two forms overlap in many places. Active participants in motorized traffic are obliged to be acquainted with the relevant traffic signals and signs. By contrast, when it comes to semipublic or private signaletics systems, the acquisition of such knowledge is optional; it's up to the individual. The latter orientation elements, which are provided in addition to normative systems, are primarily denoted today as signaletics.

Both forms basically refer to traffic routes. The signals used for this purpose need to be linguistically, visually, and acoustically coded in such a way that people can perceive them in sensory terms and decode them, i.e., understand their meaning and classify them in order of importance. Graphic symbols serve as warning signals and provide information and directional instructions, thereby facilitating orientation in traffic, in complex buildings, in large areas, and in (public) space. Being able to orient oneself is a fundamental human need. However, as Beate Kling argues, orientation does not function without independent thought and action: "As clear as guide systems may be in spatial contexts, active utilization is nevertheless required if they are to be successful."[1] Anyone who is not acquainted with the script or cultural codes of a country, for example the Arabic or Chinese alphabet or pictograms, will quickly become lost.

The signaletic information chain

Orientation design, or wayfinding—as signaletics is also referred to—structures a route from one place or space to the next in segments. The orienting chain of signs is composed of wayfinding elements (directional arrows labeled with destination information regarding an area, a building, a space, etc.) and destination confirmation (signage indicating the entrance to an area, a building, a space, etc.). At important decision-making points, such as intersections and junctions, symbols point to the next destinations. Such orientation, of course, functions best when there is a line of sight between the elements involved. Even the best signaletics system cannot completely compensate for architectural faults, such as poorly defined entrances or illogical spatial sequences.

From individual sign to system

Until well into the twentieth century, sign painters produced orientation plaques as individual pieces of (artistic) handicraft. In the course of the twentieth century, such signs were increasingly replaced by industrially manufactured and in part standardized signs. In the first quarter of the twentieth century, individual pioneers already designed more or less systematically structured orientation elements. In 1916, Edward Johnston designed a special font for the London Underground, Johnston Sans. He also created an early form of the Underground's famous circular red logo *(Roundel)*. One of the first color-coded wayfinding systems for an interior was designed by Max Burchartz in the 1920s for the Hans-Sachs-Haus in Gelsenkirchen. However, it was not until after the Second World War that hierarchically refined signaletics systems, that is, systems coordinated in thematic, visual, and constructive-material terms, became established on a large scale.

Private or public responsibility?

Over the course of the nineteenth century, public authorities—particularly in the rapidly growing cities—increasingly took over responsibility for the development of orientation elements and their legal regulation. This was not a self-evident development, and it was only after drawn-out processes of negotiation with property owners, users, and interest groups that traffic signalization as well as street naming became the preserve of state authorities.[2]

Orientation in the country and in the city

Wayfinding in the modern sense first became an issue with the construction of safe path, street, and railway networks in the nineteenth century.[3] For a long time before this, very general orientation was provided in the countryside by landmarks bearing inscriptions, such as taverns and large farms, while in towns visitors relied on signs on shops, hotels, post offices, and public institutions to find their way around. Around 1850 in New York—at the time the largest metropolis in the Western hemisphere—only a few major traffic arteries were labeled. Private property owners in good residential locations repeatedly tried to change street and place names they did not like, even painting over street signs installed by the authorities.[4] The fact that municipalities began to take control of street naming was not least a democratic act. The authorities argued that not only was it necessary to supply tourists and business travelers with the means to orient themselves, but all strata of the population should have equal access to wayfinding information.

The introduction of house numbers

One consequence of these systematizing efforts was the introduction of house numbers as abstract identifiers. Public authorities in the growing cities were looking for ways to administratively manage and document the change that was under way and decided that each property would be given a number. This facilitated the creation of property registers and the production of definitive city maps. While in many cities one can now orient oneself in the streets with the help of sequential numbers, the situation is quite different, for instance, in Japanese cities or in Venice. The postal address system in Japan is based on a plot system derived from the historic divisions between taxation districts. In Venice, all the buildings in each of the six city districts *(sestieri)* are numbered consecutively.

The increase of individual traffic

As long as movement through urban spaces was made up predominantly of pedestrians, there was no reason to hierarchize and direct traffic flows. This situation changed with the advent of industrialization and the increasing mobility of populations that accompanied it. The first individual means of transport to emerge in this context was the bicycle, which appeared at the end of the nineteenth century and which, due to the fact that it was quiet and fast, was generally regarded as dangerous. The first standardized signalization for bicycle traffic was introduced in Italy in 1880. The spread of the automobile from 1890 onward and the "danger through circulating machines"[5] this brought to urban environments created a need for commensurate signage. Early street signs were often financed by tire and automobile manufacturers, who added their own advertising ("Drive with Dunlop"). Given the divergent needs of the different stakeholders involved, this inevitably led to signage chaos.

Safety as a telling argument

In the face of this situation, city authorities realized that traffic safety could be improved for the population by systematic forms of signalization. This safety argument helped them push through standardization reforms in the face of resistance from different interest groups. It was also clear at an early stage that individual traffic would grow rapidly over the coming years and would not be confined by national borders. As early as 1903 the first pan-European conference on this topic took place. Until well into the 1960s, American and European traffic experts worked on an internationally comprehensible, standardized concept but were unable to agree on core aspects.

Signaletics as a design task

In the first half of the twentieth century, but above all after the Second World War, an ever-greater number of international regulatory systems emerged for shipping, rail, and air traffic. Intelligent, consistently designed signaletics systems that could efficiently and safely direct passenger flows became indispensable to the new complex infrastructure created for mass transportation.

At the beginning of the 1960s, street signage became a design task for the first time. The Transport font by Margaret Calvert and Jock Kinneir, and their typographic concept for British traffic signs, had a significant influence on subsequent signaletics designers. From 1960 onward, renowned designers created lettering and signaletics systems for new airports, underground rail systems, and railway stations with an emphasis on easy legibility, including from a distance. Examples include Bob Noorda's work for the Metropolitana Milanese (1964), the designs by Bob Noorda and Massimo Vignelli for the New York City subway (circa 1970), Adrian Frutiger's designs for Paris Charles de Gaulle airport (1968), and subsequent lettering styles and systems by Gerard Unger and in particular Paul Mijksenaar.

Mijksenaar and his team have designed the signage for Amsterdam Schiphol and many other airports, including those in Dallas, Rotterdam, and New York. In an interview in 2004,[6] he said that his board, color, and pictogram systems repeatedly spare passengers from having to learn new visual codes in different countries. His dream, he said, is to see as many airports as possible copy his information design. He is not alone in this hope. The search for universal-normative communication systems is particularly evident in the development of pictograms, such as those by Otl Aicher for the Olympic Games in Munich in 1972. However, in spite of the efforts of each new generation of designers to devise them, universal designs are doomed to failure in the long term because of the influence of cultural differences on perception and changes in aesthetic conceptions.

Systems in postwar modernity

Comprehensive signage also became a feature of public and semipublic buildings such as hospitals, universities, and city administrative buildings as well as private commercial buildings and areas, and it was subsequently also introduced to prestigious buildings such as museums, theaters, and libraries. The breakthrough for signaletics systems coincided with the decline of architecture-specific building signage between 1960 and 1980. This can be explained in historical and/or systemic terms. Early signaletics systems for infrastructural buildings drew on knowledge derived from traffic signalization. When designing traffic guidance systems, it was important to clearly delimit the orientation elements from their architectural environment in terms of material, color, and construction to ensure they could be easily perceived. Ignoring architecture in this explicit fashion can be termed a hands-off strategy. This approach suited the architects of postwar modernity. Their (grid-based) architectures were not supposed to be directly or prominently labeled and were deliberately designed not to display lettering. This still applies in part today.

Individualization within systematization

The last two decades have seen the further development of signaletics systems in terms of fonts and pictograms but above all with regard to materials and colors. This process has seen them to some extent adapted to the architecture they are associated with, in some cases exhibiting playful or narrative aspects that go beyond the pure provision of information. The concrete formulation of designs in this context is influenced by different factors: What type of building is involved? What is the setting in which the building is located? From whom does a commission come, to whom is it awarded, and with what objective? What specifications and contents form the basis on which the overall communication idea is developed?

Signaletics designs commissioned by users, operators, and building developers are usually functional, i.e., user-oriented. The communication idea is often derived from a firm's corporate design or the building identity, and as a result accords with marketing-technical specifications rather than territorial-architectural principles.

Information displays in public space

Since the 1980s, an increasing number of wayfinding systems for pedestrians have been installed in public space. These provide orientation for strangers and visitors by guiding users in a targeted and efficient manner to important facilities, institutions, and points of interest. The fact that municipalities are defining themselves in this way as actively communicating service providers for different user groups is in principle a welcome development. A question that has now arisen is whether in the near future some of the many information displays that currently have a physical presence in space—and often compete with other spatial installations—will be supplemented or even replaced by digital signage and exactly what form this will take.

1 Beate Kling, *Signaletik – Orientierung im Raum* (Munich: Edition Detail, 2013).
2 This development is vividly and comprehensively described by David Henkin in his book *City Reading: Written Words and Public Spaces in Antebellum New York* (New York: Columbia University Press, 1998).
3 The earliest form of street signalization on the Continent was the system of Roman milestones, which showed the distances, travel times, and directions to destinations. Stone markers were also used to indicate the boundaries of properties, municipalities, and provinces.
4 Henkin, *City Reading.*
5 Ibid.
6 *Die Zeit*, February 5, 2004.

SEEING OR READING?

THE RECEPTION OF ARCHITECTURE AND SCRIPT

Even in small dimensions, the script code is able to compete with the architectural code and even dominate it. While in terms of design and utilization, architecture and script are based on similar design-constructive principles, the ways in which they are perceived are fundamentally different.

Script is visually intelligible language. It is usually set in lines and translated via a linear reading process. The gaze has to follow the lines if the message is to be decoded. Different concepts of the reception of linear script and image- and scene-based architecture can lead to conflicts between the two media.

While most people learn the alphabetical code, this is not the case with the architectural code. Architecture cannot be "read" like a book. As in the case of images, no direction of reading is prescribed, such as from left to right or from top to bottom. Architecture is manifested as a whole, even if certain dominant elements (entrances, towers, and so on) steer our visual reception. We perceive architecture as a multidimensional totality, permanently reconciling small elements with the entirety. The longer one looks, the deeper and more detailed the impression becomes. If linear script on the facade forces its way into the foreground, it attracts the gaze to itself and away from the building.

Signage is composed of words and symbols that interact with the architecture in different ways. From the communication perspective, it remains vexing that most architects and journalists who address this topic refer to graphics, signs, and symbols indiscriminately, without categorically distinguishing between written characters and pictorial elements. Yet this distinction is central to building signage.

When, for example, script is used ornamentally, its pictorial rather than linguistic aspect constituting the focus of its expressive quality, it approaches the architecture and can be better integrated without disrupting it, even though this may in some cases detract from optimal legibility.

Part 2

28 CASE STUDIES

Project 1

NEW BUILDING KUNSTMUSEUM BASEL BASEL CH / 2016

Architecture **CHRIST & GANTENBEIN (BASEL CH)**
Media design **IART AG (BASEL CH)**

The new building for the Kunstmuseum Basel harmoniously blends in with its urban context and enters into a self-confident dialogue with the museum's original building, dating from 1936. With the idiosyncratic polygonal figure of the new structure, architects Emanuel Christ and Christoph Gantenbein have created multiple and subtle connections with the older building in terms of choice of materials, facade composition, and spatial organization. With their artful new building, the architects take up defining elements of the original building and translate them into a contemporary design idiom.

The new building can be accessed underground from the main building but also has its own entrance. This has been formed as an indented corner and refers spatially to the main facade of the original building with its arcade. The light-gray brick facade refers to the light limestone facade of the older building and exhibits a similar structure. The upper level features a frieze that runs around the entire building.

In creating this feature, the architects took the typology of sculptured friezes made up of lettering, pictures, or graphic patterns and transferred it technologically and aesthetically into the present. Their efforts have produced something seldom achieved by media (or partly mediatized) facades: a convincing solution ideally integrated into the architecture. In collaboration with the Basel-based media specialists iart, they developed a communicative frieze that combines analogue with electronic elements.

Flat, individually controllable LED profiles have been mounted on the narrow ledges created by bricks protruding 4 centimeters. Their light is optimally reflected by the chamfered bricks especially manufactured for this purpose. Due to the way they have been mounted, the profiles themselves are not visible to the observer; however, the content that is radiated by them is highly visible and legible from the street and above all from a distance. The new building has been conceived for special exhibitions, and the easy flexibility offered by the frieze is particularly well suited to the display of frequently changing exhibition information.

The frieze is able to do more than show texts and have them disappear again. Graphic patterns and pictorial figures can be represented as both positives and negatives. Static elements alternate with animated ones; at times the massive structure seems to be moving. The quantity of light can be subtly controlled; information is gently faded in and out, and highly poetic, fleeting photographic images are generated before the observer's eyes. The media frieze is a long way from the classic illuminated sign. Indeed, its aesthetic effect is such that it appears as an integral component of the brickwork.

Individually controllable LED elements have been mounted in strips on the 4-cm ledges created by the chamfered bricks. The lighting elements are 23 mm deep and 8 mm high, and were specially developed for this building.

Staff from iart check the control system on a test facade.

The shadowing effect of the chamfered joints is canceled out wherever the LEDs are activated, creating a system that can generate positive and negative renderings of lettering and graphic patterns that move across the facade.

Project 2

STÜCKI SHOPPING CENTER BASEL CH / 2009

Architecture **DIENER & DIENER ARCHITEKTEN (BASEL CH)**

Media design **IART AG (BASEL CH)**

The Stücki shopping center, opened in the Basel suburb of Kleinhüningen in 2009, is one of Switzerland's largest shopping centers and is located in a formerly industrial area. The impressive building complex was designed by the Basel-based architects Diener & Diener. Stücki comprises a mall with 120 shops, a fitness center, and a hotel offering 144 beds, over a total area of 32,000 square meters. Four high, windowless towers house the complex's technical facilities. The building is 367 meters long and 110 meters wide, and its different sections are optically knitted together by the artful use of white as a base color.

The 38-meter-high towers mark the entrances and exits to the site. Diener & Diener proposed to the building's developers that they engage the media design firm iart to develop an overall multimedia concept for the signage and lighting elements of the shopping center. The result was 15-meter-high, flush-mounted LED fields on two sides of each of the four towers. These fields recall bar codes and additionally emphasize the verticality of the towers. By night they radiate moving pictures and symbols, which contribute to shaping Basel's skyline.

The content of the light displays changes according to requirements; they are used not only to advertise brand names and products but also to display material relating to holidays or the seasons. The team from iart developed special software that enables entered content to be abstracted and matched with the LED grids. The iart firm specializes in the development of media solutions for specific spatial-constructive conditions and assists ambitious architects with the technologically integral implementation of their design ideas. The firm aims to develop solutions in which the technology is no longer perceived as detached from the overall structural aesthetic but instead coalesces with it to become a formative element. Stücki was one of the first construction projects in Switzerland to feature a media facade that satisfactorily met both technological and aesthetic criteria.

The project also illustrates the importance of coordinating all signage elements with one another and with the architecture from the outset. During the initial phase of use, it became clear that the illuminated lettering on the roof and above all the classic signage on the facade clashed with the LED frieze. The operators have now engaged the architects and the iart team to rework these elements. The result is eagerly awaited.

Stücki

Highly visible from a distance: The LED frieze looks like a barcode, which makes sense for a shopping center.

The user logos on the facade—here, partly obscured by a tree—compete with the ideally integrated media facade. This clash is currently being corrected.

Project 3

NEW YORK TIMES BUILDING NEW YORK USA / 2007

Architecture **RENZO PIANO BUILDING WORKSHOP (GENUA IT / PARIS FR)**

Typography **MICHAEL BIERUT / PENTAGRAM (NEW YORK USA)**

The new headquarters of the renowned New York Times Company in the heart of Manhattan defies superlatives. Renzo Piano Building Workshop won the star-studded invited competition in the year 2000 with its design for an elegant and unusually transparent high-rise building. The facade consists entirely of insulating glass with a low g-value (solar heat gain coefficient) and a suspended layer of horizontal, light-colored ceramic rods. This second skin protects staff against glaring sunlight and further reduces energy input. The building strives for maximum energy efficiency and yet offers the luxury of floor-to-ceiling glazing—an unresolvable contradiction.

Located in midtown Manhattan, the New York Times Building is the fifth-highest skyscraper in the city. Its 52 stories and elevation of 319 meters makes it stand out amidst New York's skyline. Its status as one of the most important pieces of corporate architecture to be undertaken in recent years prompted outstanding performances from all project partners, including the designers from the internationally acclaimed Pentagram agency tasked with the building's lettering.

Designer Michael Bierut faced the challenge of transposing the famous New York Times lettering as a sign measuring 4.5 meters by 33.5 meters onto the finely formulated facade without disturbing its expression. This difficult assignment was further complicated by the strict municipal regulations governing the size, materials, and application of logos in this historic district. The building's sun and sight protection being separated from the facade for technical reasons, and forming a veil dissolving at the corners and upward, provided Bierut with an ideal starting point for integrating the lettering into the outer skin, not only optically but also constructively.

In close association with Renzo Piano Building Workshop, Bierut and his team developed an ingenious solution. The Gothic typeface was divided into 959 small oblong pieces, which were lined up on the ceramic rods like pearls on a string. The aluminum, drop-shaped elements were slightly inclined horizontally, thus fulfilling two requirements at the same time: they offer staff a near-unimpeded outward view while the lettering is optimally legible from the street. Quite an achievement!

The New York Times
PACKAGE TOURS
LOS ANGELES
MEXICO
HAWAII PUERTO RICO
SOUTH AMERICA
MIDDLE EAST · GREEK

The headquarters of the *New York Times* is currently New York's fifth-highest building.

The view to the outside is hardly affected by the lettering mounted on the ceramic rods.

The *New York Times* lettering was cut into 959 pieces, which were mounted individually on the ceramic rods.

The New York Times

Project 4

PARKING GARAGE SANTA MONICA PLACE SANTA MONICA USA / 1980

Architecture **GEHRY PARTNERS & VICTOR GRUEN ASSOCIATES (LOS ANGELES USA)**

Typography **GEHRY PARTNERS**

Built between 1973 and 1980, the Santa Monica Place shopping mall is located at the southern end of one of the city's business districts. At the time, shopping mall concepts tried out in American suburbs were being transferred to the urban sphere. Using a clever arrangement and a full-scale volume, architect Frank Gehry and staff at Victor Gruen Associates succeeded in relating the complex to the surrounding buildings, the neighboring city district. The sophisticated interplay between cohesion and openness was also translated into the lettering of the southern car park. The lettering is very large, but the use of unobtrusive materials and weaving the letters into the shell-like facade mitigated its impact.

The architects positioned the two malls including the anchor tenants on one of the diagonals, the two parking lots on the other, a solution that contravened then-orthodox mall theories. Gehry could not identify with the developer's wishes and requirements and considered the project an unfinished work. To alleviate their hardness, the architects draped the six-story parking decks with a veil of industrial wire mesh, a "poor" material often used by Gehry.

The lettering—SANTA MONICA PLACE—covers the entire facade, measuring 100 meters in width by 8 meters in height. A small-leaning italic, bold, and narrow majuscule font was used, whose strongly geometricized form is closely related to the choice of materials. The lettering was cut out of light-colored, silver-sprayed wire mesh and applied onto the base shell. Its transparency breaks the monumentality and permits enough light to enter the parking decks behind. It is amazing that such large and pragmatic lettering can have such a magical effect—moreover, at an affordable price.

View from inside one of the parking decks through the transparent wire mesh.

Silver-sprayed wire mesh delineates the lettering from the unsprayed facade shell.

The 8-meter-high lettering faces onto the approach road and extends over the entire facade. Despite its monumental size, it remains unobtrusive.

Project 5

EXTENSION WALLRAF-RICHARTZ-MUSEUM & FONDATION CORBOUD COLOGNE DE / 2015

Architecture **CHRIST & GANTENBEIN (BASEL CH)**

Typography **LUDOVIC BALLAND (BASEL CH)**

In 2015 the Basel-based architects Emanuel Christ and Christoph Gantenbein won the competition for the extension of the Wallraf-Richartz-Museum in Cologne, and the realization of their self-confident yet restrained design is eagerly awaited.

The new building comprises a differentiated ensemble of museum spaces, apartments, and offices. To the south the structure features smaller elements which, as one walks toward Marsplatz, give way to the striking front building—the actual museum. The lively, almost archaic-looking facade composed of horizontally layered, projecting and recessed bricks of different colors and dimensions takes into account both the historical surroundings and the Ungers building from 2001.

The architects partly open up the volume of the almost closed building on the ground floor, thereby creating an inviting gesture. Through sloped supports, an outside observer can look into the interior. It is only at second glance that the expressively formed pillars—which seem to be forcing their way out of the ground—become recognizable as letters or letter fragments. Due to the powerful defamiliarization effect, it is only at third glance that concrete words come into focus (WALLRAF-RICHARTZ). The names of the collection's donors thus support the structure; their fundamental role in relation to the building becomes an element determining what the building expresses.

With their prominent use of lettering, the architects also reference the artists' names cast like reliefs in metal plates that Ian Hamilton Finlay incorporated in the basalt strips on the Ungers facade and the loosely arranged nameplates in the stairwell of the old building by the Dutch lettering designer René Knip. The latter not only designed a special font for the museum but also subtly fitted the nameplates into Ungers's joint arrangement.

To design the lettering, the architects brought in the Basel-based graphic designer Ludovic Balland, who, among other things, specializes in font design. An initial collective sketch led to close collaboration on the project. Balland's lettering has a highly constructed and robust effect. Through abstraction and fragmentation the lettering almost becomes an illegible ornament. In this way it not only conforms optically to the architecture but through its tectonic formation becomes fully integrated in it.

Balland has already worked with the architects on various projects; however, this intensive engagement with lettering in the building process is new for him. According to Balland, a generational change is under way: young architectural firms respect the work of graphic designers in a new way and are involving them at an early stage—as in the case of the project discussed here—in the architectural design process.

The "tectonically" formed lettering plinth spells out the names of the museum's founding donors: Wallraf–Richartz.

Project 6

E,D,E,N PAVILION HOTEL EDEN RHEINFELDEN CH / 1987

Architecture **HERZOG & DE MEURON (BASEL CH)**

Typography **HERZOG & DE MEURON**

The small sculptural structure by the architects Jacques Herzog and Pierre de Meuron stands amidst beautiful old trees in the grounds of the Hotel Eden in Rheinfelden. An encounter with the structure while strolling in the grounds is initially an unsettling experience in the most pleasant sense. Four idiosyncratically formed pillars support a rigid, flat concrete roof with square perforations in it. Closer inspection reveals the subtle qualities of the gazebo, the elements of which are made of blackened poured concrete. The trunks, which support a roof of foliage stylized as an abstract grid, reveal themselves as letters: *E*, *D*, *E*, and *N*. The letter pillars are an integral element of the structure and each of them expresses a different relationship to the roof above. The central horizontal bars of the *E*s are positioned in the mathematical rather than the typographical middle, which lends them a tectonic quality. The *D* with its belly seems to be bending under its load, and the *N* appears split. It is as if the roof is holding the supports in place and trying to prevent them from leaping away. The letters are extremely narrow and high, and alternate between legibility and abstraction. This arouses curiosity and compels the observer to move, because the whole word can only be read from one particular perspective. The name EDEN is programmatic; however, the term triggers such broad associations that it becomes pure poetry. We know we are in Rheinfelden but at the same time feel a little bit as though we are in paradise.

The four pillars supporting the roof of the pavilion are formed as elongated letters *(E, D, E, N)*.

Project 7

RAIFFEISENBANK NÄFELS CH / 2012

Architecture **LUSSI + HALTER (LUCERNE CH)**
Typography **VELVET CREATIVE OFFICE (LUCERNE CH)**

This subtle design by the Lucerne architectural firm Lussi + Halter called for equally restrained signage and, happily, the Raiffeisenbank in Näfels agreed. The new bank building is part of an ensemble of residential buildings which—surrounded by stately buildings—is assuming the function of a town center in the newer part of Näfels. The solid volume of the building establishes a clear accent toward the street and protects the courtyard area at the back. Different factors contribute to the dignified character of the development: the precise positioning of the structure, the careful design of the exterior space, the artificial-stone window casements, and the rough-trowel finish and carefully coordinated colors of the facade. The different sections of the bank building come together on the ground floor, and the outer edges on this level feature a part of the word RAIFFEISEN. The effect is to bring the various structural elements together as a unified whole.

The two sections of story-high lettering are in keeping with the intention of the architecture, exhibiting large dimensions while remaining restrained. Early visualizations by the architects already featured lettering in the plinth area. To design a precise typography, they enlisted the help of the Lucerne communication and design agency Velvet. The Corporate typeface used by Raiffeisen is based on a classic Frutiger font with a special *R*, truncated horizontals on *E* and *F*, and curved ends on *A* and *N*. Like every logo, it is very much a reflection of its time. However, lettering milled into natural stone needs to be somewhat more timeless, particularly when it comes to color. The lettering was cut 5 millimeters into large, light-colored limestone slabs, which were mounted on site.

It was precisely the slightly anachronistic idea of cutting a corporate logo into stone that excited the designer and the architects. It was important to them that the facade lettering be an integral part of the design. The symbols were to age with the building, so that both would remain witnesses to the time of their creation, even if the use of the building were to change at some time in the future. The fact that architecture can be an expression of a specific corporate culture is generally well-known; the idea that lettering appropriate to that culture can support this expression is less so. As the project's client, the Raiffeisenbank in Näfels has facilitated an example that is worthy of imitation.

RA

During the design process, the Velvet design agency experimented with different typefaces in different sizes and arrangements and ultimately decided on a bold Frutiger font.

Part of the lettering cut into stone slabs to the height of the plinth on site.

Two lines of lettering visually connect the structural volumes on the ground floor. The client did not insist on having the current logotype mounted on the facade, thereby allowing for a solution that can age along with the building.

Project 8

HOTEL LOUIS MUNICH DE / 2009

Architecture **HILD UND K ARCHITEKTEN (MUNICH DE)**

Typography **HILD UND K ARCHITEKTEN**

The conversion of an administration building on Munich's famous Viktualienmarkt square into a boutique hotel with a shopping arcade presented the architects Hild und K with the task of mediating between different buildings in the context of the historic city center. They decided to approach this task by reinterpreting different Munich building traditions, the Baroque and the architecture typical of German reconstruction during the 1950s, both of which are conspicuously represented by the directly adjacent buildings. The architects' concept interweaves both styles. The hotel's regular arrangement of ceiling-high windows with French balconies lends the facade a modern character, while stucco moldings around the window apertures create a sense of Baroque dynamism.

Letters 1.9 meters high and 1.4 meters wide spell out the word HOTEL on the facade. They have been deployed as blind windows, as it were, and help to harmonize the rhythm of the facade. Significantly, the five letters do not correspond with the lines formed by the surrounding four floors. They have been inserted as a vertically staggered element at a right angle to the horizontal progression—in the direction of reading—of the windows; this artful compositional measure generates a subtle tension.

The fact that the lettering became an integral part of the facade design determined its concrete graphic form. Also designed by Hild und K, the letters exhibit—in particular in the case of the O—a highly geometric character. The dimensions of the letters correspond to those of the window apertures, which allows for optimal incorporation of the lettering into the facade structure, although using the services of a typographer might have resulted in more artfully formed letters. The letters' negative form was produced by recessing the final rendering, by using different thicknesses. The architects' choice of unusual dimensions and typography has enabled them to transfer the typology of traditionally chiseled building inscriptions into the modern context.

Compared with the specification of the use of the building (HOTEL), the name of the hotel (LOUIS) on the facade is significantly smaller, as if it were a footnote. Is this to allow for the possibility of a rapid change of ownership? On the contrary, the owners of the Hotel Louis see themselves as committed to the tradition of hospitality, and for this reason abstained from having the name of the host displayed prominently on the building.

The building's use (hotel) has been integrally "inscribed" into the facade. The name of the operator (Louis) has been added in small, very restrained shadowed lettering.

Project 9

MUNICIPAL POOLS POVOAÇÃO PT / 2008

Architecture **BARBOSA & GUIMARÃES ARQUITECTOS (MATOSINHOS PT)**

Typography **BARBOSA & GUIMARÃES ARQUITECTOS**

The village of Povoação lies at the southern tip of San Miguel, the largest island of the Azores. The municipal authorities had already cut out and leveled a site for different kinds of sports from the gently sloping hillside when Portuguese architects Barbosa & Guimaràes were commissioned to build a public swimming pool.

The architects accommodated the site's various uses in several long-shaped buildings. These volumes were positioned on, or rather inserted into, the hillside by covering the roof entirely with soil and grass. Skylights fitted into this natural covering provide good lighting in the rooms below and symbolize the artificial intervention into the landscape.

The fact that this approach also informed the design of the signage on the building, which looks as if it has been cast into the landscape, was a logical step for the architects, who regard clear and integral identification as a necessity for every public building. Their design—which was planned from the beginning of the project—refers to classical relief inscriptions chiseled into stone yet translates this technique into the modern context in graphic and material terms.

A positive relief of the lettering was mounted onto the reverse side of the formwork and cast into concrete on site, thereby producing the negative relief. In a second step, the facade was rendered using a material containing basalt. San Miguel is a volcanic island, as the unusually dark facade reminds the viewer.

Barbosa & Guimarães positioned the lettering—COMPLEXO DE PISCINAS COBERTAS DE MUNICÍPIO DA POVOAÇÃO—on the surface next to the entrance. They designed a special typeface that recalls the Portuguese lettering culture of the 1920s. The omission of the counters of some letters produced an idiosyncratic lettering. Its positioning within the predefined field—the letterspacing—followed strict mathematical principles and, aside from a few details, has been carefully executed. Yet what escapes the layperson catches the eye of the professional graphic designer; consulting a typographer would have helped eliminate some small flaws.

CO
MU
PO

The lettering was cast on site in the concrete entrance facade, which was then rendered with a roughcast containing basalt.

With roofs covered with earth and grass, the ensemble nestles into its surroundings. The lettering was part of the architectural concept from the outset.

Project 10

MASJID AL-IRSYAD KOTA BARU PARAHYANGAN PADALARANG ID / 2010

Architecture **PT. URBANE INDONESIA (BANDUNG ID)**

Typography **PT. URBANE INDONESIA**

The layout and the cubage of the buildings designed by Urbane, an Indonesian architectural firm specializing in commercial buildings, urban design, and also mosque architecture, follow a fairly simple pattern. The building volume forms a square, is closed on three sides, and opens out onto a pond on the fourth side. This structure satisfies the classical requirements of mosque architecture on the one hand, but is characterized by the absence of a dome on the other. The architects point out that domes are not an essential part of the cultural and religious identity of Islam. Its refutation of any historical reminiscence lends the building a modern appearance, without, however, neglecting the most important structural element of sacred buildings in the Islamic world, namely, the orientation toward *Ka'bah* (Mecca). The minaret is not integrated into the building, but stands to one side of the principal structure. The building is attached to its Islamic school complex within the area.

The building perfectly fulfills its purpose. Muslims pray in straight rows, each running parallel to the direction of prayer *(Qiblah)*. The mosque offers a thousand worshippers a sheltered interior, but also establishes various relationships with the outside world. The space is used for different religious ceremonies. The view across the water basin has been designed to ensure that individual worshippers can engage in intimate, contemplative prayer. The surrounding water basin also regulates temperatures during periods of hot weather.

The facade is modular and comprises various specially manufactured types of brick. Light-colored solid bricks support the building, while dark, frame-shaped stone elements pervade it. These open elements ventilate the building while also spelling out large letters. The lettering covers the building's entire outer shell. The integral words, "There is no god but God. Muhammad is the messenger of God." merge with the facade and plainly express its function; they identify the building as a house of prayer. Clearly visible from afar, the lettering summons worshippers to prayer.

The lettering forms a "veil" that mediates between inside and outside.

Light-colored solid bricks are interspersed with dark perforated ones. The combination of these two elements produces the lettering while also providing optimal ventilation for the mosque.

The lettering making up the statement "There is no god but God. Muhammad is the messenger of God." runs around the structure. It clearly expresses the building's function and is visible from afar.

Project 11

THE LYON HOUSEMUSEUM MELBOURNE AU / 2009

Architecture **LYONS ARCHITECTS (MELBOURNE AU)**

Typography **CORBETT LYON (MELBOURNE AU)**

Digital media—such as outdoor screens—are rendering large third-party advertising permanently installed on facades increasingly less legitimate. This is in sharp contrast to building lettering, tailored to a building's long-term purpose. Such lettering has been undergoing a worldwide renaissance for some years. One example is the Lyon Housemuseum in Kew, a suburb of Melbourne.

It might be objected that this building requires no lettering, as it is located in a residential district and surrounded by private homes. But this residence-cum-public museum (at least on weekdays) raises the question of how its hybrid character can be subtly communicated. The low-key solution discussed here became possible only because the architect Corbett Lyon was also the museum owner and developer. He realized that a large, shrill gesture in this location would be inappropriate.

As is common with many suburban houses, the Lyon Housemuseum is surrounded by a brick wall. Stone boundaries usually separate private from public land and have an exclusionary effect. This interface is the starting point for Lyon's design. Brick walls, being modular and consisting of layered elements, permit information to be woven into the structure using a simple procedure: some bricks project more from the wall than others and thus form a visible contrast. This creates patterns, or in this case lettering. Corbett Lyon's design thus embraces, and updates, one of the oldest lettering methods.

It seems astonishing, at first, that it is not the museum's name that has been worked into the 2.5-meter-high wall, but those of the two streets on which the museum is located. Instead of identifying the building, the letters emphasize its location in the urban body and thus provide orientation. In turn, their unusual size gives them prominence, and signals, both subtly and clearly, that this is a special building situated here. Lyon's communicative gesture somewhat dispels the wall's forbidding aspect. The simultaneously low-key and inviting spelling out of the boundary corresponds exactly to the project's hybrid character, which cuts a groove between the private and the public, art and life, architecture and art.

The Lyon Housemuseum is home to architect Corbett Lyon's superb collection of contemporary Australian art and is located in the Melbourne suburb of Kew. Protruding bricks in the wall form the names of the streets on which the museum is located.

HOTEL CITY GARDEN
ZUG CH / 2009

(ZURICH CH)

Typography **BRINGOLF IRION VÖGELI GMBH (ZURICH CH)**

The architects from EM2N and the graphic designers from Bringolf Irion Vögeli have been working together for several years with the aim of creating signage that accords with architectural intention. A good example of this aspiration is the Hotel City Garden project in Zug.

Commissioned as an ancillary hotel by the city's Parkhotel and with a planned lifespan of only twelve to fifteen years, the building was designed and built by the architects Daniel Niggli and Mathias Müller in 2008–9. The building concept is based on a series of wood frame modules (twenty-four rooms per floor) with a floor slab and vertical access core made of concrete. It was only due to the efficiency afforded by building in timber, both in terms of prefabrication and during assembly on the construction site, that it was possible to keep to the tight schedule required.

Although the building was to be designed for temporary use and it was specified that construction should be as cost-effective as possible, the hotel nevertheless had to meet the infrastructural and above all prestige requirements of a four-star establishment. The rooms are uncharacteristically arranged not orthogonally but at an angle to one another, which results in an expressive, staggered building volume. The facade is chrome-plated, lending it a noble quality, and reflects the beautiful trees in the park on one side.

By day, the front and edges of the lettering on the building have the same chrome appearance as their background. The surface is covered with a special foil that is translucent by night. The lettering reacts congenially in both optical and material terms to the architectural design and has a self-evident quality that makes it seem as if it had been part of the design from the outset.

The external lettering folds out of the facade at exactly the same angle as the room arrangement in the floor plan. This is also the case with the internal doors, on which the three-digit reflective room numbers also protrude at an angle.

The particular quality of this approach to signage is that it additionally strengthens the building's inherent dynamic. The letters seem to move out from the facade and the doors toward the observer, who stands astonished in front of them.

CITY
GARDEN

The lettering folds out of the reflective facade at exactly the same angle as the room arrangement in the floor plan.

The designers always work with handmade models in order to examine the spatial effect and materialization of their designs.

Like the facade, the edges of the letters are reflective. The special foil covering the front of the letters is translucent by night, which allows the lettering to be lit in dazzling light once darkness falls.

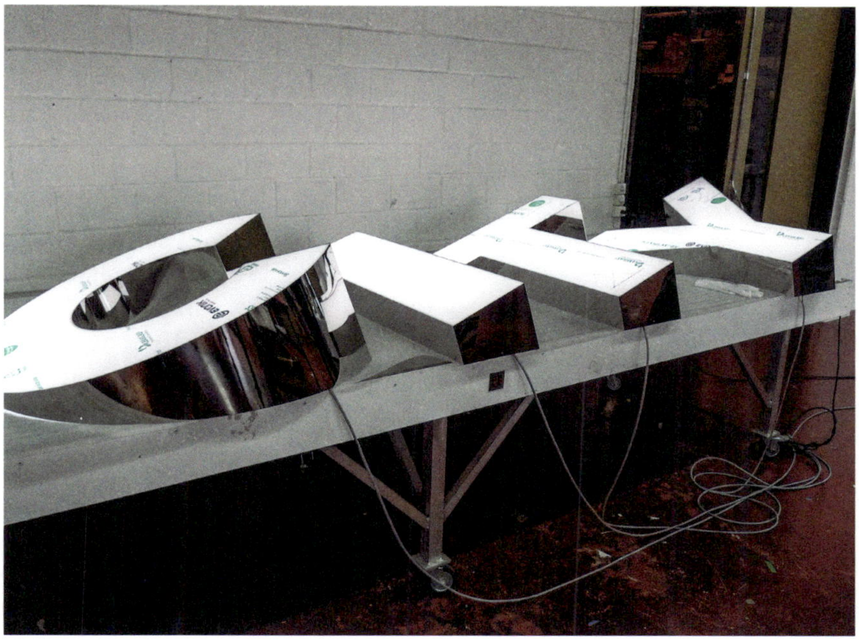

Project 13

TONI-AREAL ZURICH CH / 2014

Architecture	**EM2N ARCHITEKTEN (ZURICH CH)**
Typography	**BRINGOLF IRION VÖGELI GMBH (ZURICH CH) / HI – VISUELLE GESTALTUNG (LUCERNE CH)**
Lettering design	"Areal" font: Biv/Hi in collaboration with binnenland.ch
Product design	"Förrlibuck" sign set: Design collective Biv/Hi with David Weisser, fokusform (Zurich, CH)

The suggestion of movement created by the City Garden lettering [p. 84] can also be observed in the project undertaken by the design collective BIV Grafik/Hi – Visuelle Gestaltung with the architectural firm EM2N for the Toni-Areal in Zurich. Both projects began around the same time, although with different objectives, architectural starting points, and dimensions.

The Toni-Areal is a 24,000-square-meter area in the western part of the city of Zurich that was formerly the site of a milk factory. Between 2008 and 2014[1] the EM2N architects Daniel Niggli and Mathias Müller converted and developed the milk production plant into a university campus for five thousand students, lecturers, and staff. This campus brings together the Zurich University of the Arts (ZHdK) and a part of the Zurich University of Applied Sciences (ZHAW) as well as the Zurich Museum of Design, with its display repository. However, the design requirements also included different spaces for cultural and other events, food outlets, shops, and one hundred apartments.

The building volume of 493,400 cubic meters corresponds to that of an entire urban quarter, and the architects therefore approached the undertaking more as an urban developmental project than an architectural task. They designed the inside of the building as a complex system of halls, interior streets, intimate spaces, and cascades, creating an interior urbanism: the building as city, the city as building.

Orientation within this complex spatial structure is anything but simple, and once again the signaletics specialists from Bringolf Irion Vögeli and Hi – Visuelle Gestaltung were called in to devise an effective system. In contrast to other projects, they first designed the nearly 2-meter-high letters that mark the main access axes. The monumental letters, which are painted black on the front, exhibit a number of tectonic folds and appear to press into the walls or to be extruded from them. These letters, with their complex reliefs, invest the walls with a dynamic. The project's authors go even further and describe the letters as actors with whom students, lecturers, and visitors come into bodily contact.

At the main entrance, located on the southern side, and on the northern facade, large external signage has been installed, which is lit white at light. The multiple-folded fronts of the letters are covered with a grid foil that appears black by day but is translucent by night. Other signage—for instance for the bistro, the cinema, and the concert hall—has been coordinated with the respective background material.

1 Study: 2005; planning phase: 2005–2011; construction phase: 2008–2014

TONI-
AREAL

Bringing movement to the building: the multiply folded letters at the main entrance. This type of lettering is used on the outside of the building and for the main access axes inside it.

The almost 2-meter-high metal letters were mounted and painted black on site.

A particularly large number of models were required to check and optimize the letters' complex angle of inclination.

Lettering in the interior is in the same color and/or material as its respective background.

Mounting the complexly constructed external signage.

The designers developed the “Areal” typeface in collaboration with font designers from Binnenland.

Project 14

ROAD TRANSPORT HALL, MUSEUM OF TRANSPORT LUCERNE CH / 2009

Architecture **GIGON/GUYER ARCHITEKTEN (ZURICH CH)**

Facade design **GIGON/GUYER ARCHITEKTEN**

The Road Transport Hall, which was built for the Swiss Museum of Transport, was conceived as an exhibition building for cars, motorbikes, trucks, and bicycles. It houses a multilevel storage facility containing over forty vehicles, which can individually be brought closer to visitors by a robot. Different islands created by various designers and devoted to themes such as mobility and accident prevention provide information about road transport today and present visions of its future development.

The simple cube has two floors and an exhibition area of 2000 square meters. A central concern of the Zurich architects Annette Gigon and Mike Guyer was to have the exterior of the building express its function. The architects report that their original conception involved a facade composed of flattened car bodies. As the design process developed, they came up with the idea of cladding the outside of the building with traffic signs from Switzerland and in part from abroad, which, with their memorable typography, colors, and mass, possess an enormous visual power.

The signs were sorted according to color (green for freeways, blue for main roads, and white for side roads) and attached to different sides of the facade. On the fourth, back side, the signs were mounted in reverse so that the view from the neighboring buildings at the rear corresponds to what drivers see when approaching from the other direction.

The original idea was to install used signs. However, in the end these were used only for the signs mounted in reverse on the back of the building, because the incumbent museum director was able to negotiate a very good deal with a supplier of brand new signs.

The resulting facade explicitly communicates the use of the building. It can be interpreted as an ironic variation on the decorated shed as defined in the 1970s by American architects Robert Venturi, Denise Scott Brown & Associates.

In this case, however, a faceless building volume is not structurally separated from a dominant layer of symbols. Instead, the typographic skin coincides in a materially and communicatively integral and thus congenial way with the content of the building.

A congenial melding of expression and content. The facade of the Road Transport Hall is completely covered with street signs.

Project 15

GAS RECEIVING STATION DINTELOORD NL / 2013

Architecture **STUDIO MARCO VERMEULEN (ROTTERDAM NL)**

Typography **STUDIO MARCO VERMEULEN**

With fossil fuels becoming scarcer, new technologies capable of simplifying production cycles and using local resources are becoming more important. The New Prinsenland intensive agricultural and food production cluster in Dinteloord, 50 kilometers south of Rotterdam, points the way toward post-fossil production. One of the facility's hallmarks is the production of biogas from vegetable and sugarcane wastes. The modest building from which this gas is fed into the grid was the starting point for researching new materials and their use in the construction industry.

The building with its unusual facade panels was designed by the Dutch architect Marco Vermeulen, who used *Nabasco*, a building material developed by the Haarlem-based firm NPSP which consists of a mixture of *bio-resin*—a non-toxic *plastic* based on renewable raw materials—and *hemp fibers*. The development of such biodegradable materials is still in its fledgling stages but is bound to markedly affect the future of the construction industry.

The above-ground building volume, with its simple cubage, provides no indication of the complex underground network of gas lines, tunnels, and infrastructure. Vermeulen's Nabasco panels are the world's first-ever facade made from biologically processed and fully recyclable materials.

Vermeulen integrated the chemical formula for biogas directly into the panel-casting process. The differently sized letters *H* (hydrogen), *C* (carbon), and *N* (nitrogen) form a typographical pattern that stands out as a positive relief. This cleverly conveys—albeit in a slightly encoded form—the building's purpose. While joint distribution and panel fastening remain visible, they are optically dominated by the overall typographical relief.

The glossy brown facade, reminiscent of chocolate, may appear a peculiar choice. Keen to distinguish it from "eco-aesthetics," Vermeulen gave the facade an explicitly inorganic look. The "mouthwatering" effect is a reference to the nearby sugar refinery. Originally, Vermeulen had considered using sugar-based bioresin, but this idea was too far ahead of its time.

The letters *H*, *C*, and *N* compose the chemical formula for biogas. The typographical relief covering the facade subtly expresses the building's function.

Casting mold for the individual letters and facade panels.

This facade could be composted. It consists of a mixture of bioresin—a nontoxic plastic gained from renewable raw materials—and hemp fibers.

Project 16

CORPORATE DESIGN FOR SMALL BUILDINGS ZURICH CH / 2004[1]

Architecture **KAUFMANN WIDRIG ARCHITEKTEN GMBH (ZURICH CH)**

Typography **AGNÈS LAUBE (ZURICH CH)**

In 2004 the City of Zurich held a competition to find a corporate design for its small buildings: boathouses, kiosks, and toilet facilities in public space. The Zurich architects Daniel Kaufmann and Michael Widrig submitted an idea for a series of buildings that they developed together with the Zurich graphic designer Agnès Laube. Central to the development of their concept was the question of how these buildings in public space could be lent a shared architectural aesthetic while also distinguishing between their respective uses and locations. It quickly became clear to the interdisciplinary team, which had been working in the field of archigraphy under the name of Arge L-KW since 2002, that lettering would play a defining role in this project.

The architectural concept envisaged relating the small buildings to one another by way of a basic volumetric typology. This was to consist of clearly legible, simple types of layout—with asymmetrically formed roofs that clarified the focus of the building within its urban environment. This repeated form was to be contextualized by varying the materials used for the roof and the entire facade.

Agnès Laube designed a typographic ornament consisting of a sequence that repeated and pushed together the letters *Z* and *H*—the abbreviation for Zurich. This pattern was to cover the entire outside of the buildings—like the initials on a Louis Vuitton bag—thereby underscoring the idea of a corporate architecture and unobtrusively identifying the City of Zurich as the builder. The team experimented with different metals such as bronze, brass, and chromium steel and with ways of applying the lettering over the entire surface using techniques such as black-finishing, etching, and sandblasting.

Rather than carving the letters out of the facade or applying them to it, the designers found it more interesting in this case to transform the metal skin using thermal or chemical processes. The result was a basic symbolic identifier which—supplemented by functional signage—is intended as a tongue-in-cheek nod to trendy corporate design concepts.

1 2nd prize, unbuilt

ZH13013

The project required intensive experimentation with different processes (e.g., anodization, black-finishing) that could be used to apply the lettering ornament *ZH* (standing for Zurich) to the chromium steel, brass, and bronze surfaces of the small buildings.

Different facing materials were used to contextualize the small buildings—which are based on a standard structural type—and integrate them within the urban environment. Here we see the shimmering silver variation used for the kiosks.

Project 17

RAKETE
BASEL CH / 2012

Architecture **BAUBÜRO IN SITU / NRS-TEAM (BASEL CH / ZURICH CH)**

Typography **HAUSER, SCHWARZ (BASEL CH)**

Since 2012 there has been a space station of sorts in Basel. From here young designers blast off into the universe of the creative economy. In order to ensure that their launch into the realm of entrepreneurship is as successful as possible, they are provided with support from the Basel-based Christoph Merian Foundation, which initiated and financed the studio building. Studio spaces in the building are not subsidized by the foundation. However, because construction costs were kept low, rents are very moderate. The infrastructure is simple but adequate, and the surrounding Dreispitz area is highly inspiring.

The thirty-two studios are available for use for ten years and—like the "Basislager" opened in Zurich on a disused industrial site in 2009—were constructed using standard containers as modules. However, in Basel the container building was gently refined—in part through the application of a coat of anthracite-colored paint—which is in keeping with the structure's partly representative function. The studio building forms the entrance to the Dreispitz area, which is one of the largest development projects in Switzerland. A model of the transformation of the area is on display on the ground floor, and visitors can monitor the state of the project with their own eyes from a 17-meter-high viewing tower.

The architects from NRS-team GmbH emphasized the temporary character of the complex by constructing the stairs and pathways out of standard scaffolding covered with wire netting and leaving all piping and installations visible. The Basel design duo of Simon Hauser and David Schwarz took up this architectural idea and used it to develop concise illuminated lettering—and an entire corporate design program.

Drawing on the visual dominance of the scaffolding poles on the building, they also used these for the frame supporting the main sign and echoed the modular character of the container structure in the way they framed each of the characters. These two elements form a visual building-block system from which all other applications (website, printed materials, etc.) can be derived.

The front of the illuminated letters and the first 5 centimeters of the 12-centimeter-deep edges are colored with anthracite paint. Light is emitted from the remaining 7 centimeters of the edges and from the back, which serves to emphasize the white-painted supporting frame. As a result, the frame—an element usually accepted as a necessary evil—becomes the star of the show, exuding an almost magical aura.

Finally, we come to an aspect that was there from the very beginning of the project: the name. The somewhat nostalgic term *Rakate*, or rocket, was one (actually the first) of 150 proposed names, which were evaluated within the foundation and at times heatedly discussed. The fact that the designers were able to devise lettering that congenially presented the name in visual and constructive terms contributed to its ultimate acceptance. Sometimes combustive ideas need time before they can assert themselves—and above all a lot of space.

The designers decided to embrace the situation they were facing and, rather than try to conceal the scaffolding, gave it a key role in their signage solution. The result fits well with the studio building, which is made up of building containers and standard scaffolding.

Light is emitted from the back of the letters, giving the white-painted supporting structure even more prominence by night.

The magical effect first becomes evident when a dark- or light-colored metal is used.

Testing a prototype on site with a crane.

View into the interior of a letter body with LEDs in place.

The designers derived a corporate design system for the entire "Rakete" project (logo, interior wayfinding, business stationery, etc.) from the appearance of the main signage.

Project 18

BUCHWIESEN SCHOOL ZURICH CH / 2004

Architecture **ARNOLD AMSLER (WINTERTHUR CH)**

Art work **MARIO SALA (WINTERTHUR CH)**

Buchwiesen School is located on the northern edge of the city of Zurich in the Seebach district. Postwar urban development was dominated by the idea of the green and leafy garden city, and it was this concept that shaped the approach of the architects who designed the school complex at Buchwiesen 1–3 in the 1950s. In 2002 the architect Arnold Amsler replaced a part of the school with a new structure. The resulting three-story, wood-clad wing and the gymnasium with a PVC facade contrast starkly with the restrained scale of the surrounding buildings and bring new visual elements to the area.

The Swiss artist Mario Sala, who was commissioned to contribute a construction art piece entitled *Airport* to the building project, drew on the qualities of the location and their contradictions and exaggerated them. Two-meter-high letters on the roof form the words WILLKOMMEN IN BUCHWIESEN ("Welcome to Buchwiesen"). Sala appropriates the architecture of the school building and tells stories: stories of migration and minimally equipped airfields on other continents; stories of urban-fringe and industrial areas undergoing rapid change, of their abrupt alterations in scale and screaming advertising signs. He also brings a touch of the past glamour of Hollywood to a modest suburban neighborhood in the Zurich airport corridor.

Flying is referenced here in a multilayered way. In a positive sense, airplanes in the sky belong to dreams of travel, are part of memories, and awaken desires. On the other hand, aircraft noise is a significant problem for the area. The proportion of foreigners making up the population of such negatively impacted neighborhoods is often very high, and the composition of classes at the school is accordingly multicultural.

Arriving and departing: these themes are also central ones for a school. Pupils from different cultures encounter one another here, spending a part of their great learning journey together and then moving on. Irrespective of their origins, all of them should be made warmly welcome during their time at Buchwiesen School. The outsized roof signage could hardly make this any clearer. But is it only the children and young people attending the school who are being addressed by this message?

In relation to the building volume, the white lettering is oversized and as a result is initially unsettling. The letters are cut from simple tin plate and mounted on a frame painted in a luminous red. As a result, the overall effect of the lettering is somewhat cheap and makeshift. Sala's intervention is superficially loud and cheerful but at the same time seems temporary and thus precarious. The neighborhood population and aircraft passengers are given a big and promising welcome to Buchwiesen, and yet it is a promise that comes off as oddly empty.

BU

The artist Mario Sala has given the supporting frame a prominent role. In material terms, his lettering appears somewhat impoverished compared with other examples in Switzerland, a strategy intended to refer to more "precarious" locations elsewhere in the world.

Construction-art lettering as critical-ironic commentary. The welcome is directed not only at pupils of the school but also at passengers in the planes thundering overhead. The building lies in the approach corridor of Zurich airport.

Project 19

DISTRICT GOVERNMENT BUILDING DIETIKON CH / 2010

Architecture **ANDREAS SENN ARCHITEKTUR (ST. GALLEN CH)**

Typography **BRINGOLF IRION VÖGELI GMBH (ZURICH CH)**

The sharp-edged concrete cube was already finished when the designers from the firm of Bringolf Irion Vögeli GmbH first stepped onto the building site. The competition for the design of a new building for the Dietikon district government had been won by the architectural office Andreas Senn from St. Gallen back in 1998. However, it was not until 2010 that the building was inaugurated. The twelve-year process of constructing the building, which needed to combine very different uses under one roof (cantonal police, district attorney, district court, district prison, and district administration), was marked by several revisions and difficult conditions. What is astonishing is that, despite a long planning phase, the signage and wayfinding systems for this public building were all but forgotten.

The building volume is made up of two interlocked right-angle sections that together create three different building heights. This double L-form creates an interior open-top courtyard. The character of the building's exterior is shaped by the exposed concrete facade featuring recessed ribbon windows. The lettering designers countered the strict orthogonal architecture by using a font with a soft character: Brauer Neue. The typeface was designed in 1974 by the Zurich graphic designer Pierre Miedinger as a corporate font for the Hürlimann brewery. Starting in 1999 it was digitalized by a young graphic designer and developed into a font family.

The materials used for the building formed the point of departure for the signage concept. The signaletics designers suggested using letters made of concrete for both the building's name, displayed prominently on the front side, and the interior signage on the different floors; for the signage on the doors made of European chestnut, they proposed using the same type of wood. One of the firm's specialties is its enthusiastic experimentation with volumes and materials until a building-specific solution has been found. Ideas are tested using handmade models, and construction variants are discussed with specialists.

In this project, much of the signage is three-dimensional, which, depending on the angle of view, creates a lively play of light and shadow without negatively influencing legibility. This is particularly evident in the case of the signage on the different floors. All the floors are listed on each level. However, the concrete letters identifying the floor one is on protrude slightly farther than the others. The observer not only sees the signage but also senses it physically. These solutions seem so self-evident that it is as if they were planned from the beginning. Moreover, they lend this rather rigorous building a friendly face.

BEZIRKSGEBÄUDE DIETIKON

Different depths of lettering are used in the interior floor signage to literally foreground the location of the observer.

The “Brauer” typeface was designed by Pierre Miedinger in 1974 for the Hürlimann brewery. Starting in 1996, Philippe Desarzens digitalized the typeface and developed it into a font family.

The letters were cast in concrete and mounted on the facade. Their appearance creates the impression that they were planned from the beginning and lends a friendly face to the sharp-edged building.

The letters making up the interior floor signage were milled out of cast concrete slabs.

Project 20

PRIMARY SCHOOL WITH PUBLIC LIBRARY DIETLIKON CH / 2013

Architecture **BAUMBERGER & STEGMEIER AG (ZURICH CH)**
Typography **BAUMBERGER & STEGMEIER AG**

Dietlikon is a typical agglomeration municipality near Zurich, not far from the city's airport. Its appearance is shaped by specialist retailers and sales businesses, and like many villages in this area it grew significantly in the 1960s. The community of just under seven thousand residents is proud of its intact village center, which is lovingly cared for.

This is witnessed by the new, painstakingly designed primary school with an integrated public library, which is located on the edge of the village center. The architects Peter Baumberger and Karin Stegmeier have slightly bent the 50-meter-long two-story building in the middle. With its delicately structured facade, the building thus interpolates itself into the scale of its surroundings and forms a new, convincing unity with the older building stock. The conspicuously protruding roof protects the entrance area from wind and rain, forming a useful outside meeting area for the pupils. The light gray wood coating lends the building—together with the projecting roof—the air of a contemporary public structure.

The library, which is located on the upper floor on the southern side, is prominently marked by large exterior lettering. From the outset the architects approached this signage as an integral design element in terms of material, color, and visual impact. By precisely positioning the lettering, the architects have simultaneously solved a number of problems: the location is identified, an elegant transition is created between the floors, the corner location is resolved, and the entrance area is optically enlarged.

The height and width of the lettering is defined by the loadbearing structure and the layout of the architecture. In order to fit the lettering into the field available for it, the architects simply had to find an appropriate high and narrow font. After extensive research they ultimately decided on Catorze27 by the Portuguese font designer Fabio Duarte Martins, which fits well with the spirit of the project.

The 1.5-meter-high sign is made of aluminum, which is cheaper and more weatherproof than wood. The font was slightly revised for this particular application: the width of a number of letters was reduced and the vertical strokes exhibit the same width as the wood slats on the facade. As a whole the lettering is generally well spaced, which cannot be taken for granted when architects do their own typographic design.

It is above all due to the initiative taken by the architects themselves that the signage here appears to be such an integral element of this building with its delicate and airy character. The fact that only limited resources were available is not evident in the solution that has been found. On the contrary, the project is a good example of how attractive and original signage can be created on a restricted budget.

By precisely positioning the lettering, the architects have simultaneously solved a number of problems: the location of the library is identified, an elegant transition is created between the floors, the corner location is resolved, and the entrance area is optically enlarged. The fine lettering has been fitted into a field measuring 1.5 by 5.4 meters and has a depth of 80 mm.

The "Catorze27" typeface was designed by the Portuguese font designer Fabio Duarte Martins in 2011. He was inspired by the building signage forged by northern Portuguese artisans in the 1950s.

Project 21

RBC DESIGN CENTER MONTPELLIER FR / 2012

Architecture **ATELIERS JEAN NOUVEL (PARIS FR) WITH C+D ARCHITECTURE (MONTPELLIER FR)**

Typography **ATELIERS JEAN NOUVEL WITH L'AUTOBUS IMPÉRIAL**

Part of the concept of Franck Argentin—whose company RBC distributes furniture conceived by internationally acclaimed designers—is to have equally famous architects build his showrooms. One example is Jean Nouvel's design for the RBC Design Center in Montpellier. The building is located on an arterial road in the city's new Port Marianne business district.

Seen from the street, the broad approach zone conveys a sense of the building's whole site. Nouvel makes paradoxical use of this feature by downplaying the street-facing facade and turning the two facades running perpendicularly to the street into *display facades*, indeed into proper *commercial facades*. Behind the metal trellises, the street facade reveals the building's technical structure: various escape platforms and stairs accessible from eight mezzanine-type exhibition levels.

Above the glazed ground floor, gray beams clad with profile sheets divide the main facades almost from top to bottom. Narrow, horizontal window slits allude to the upper stories. Slightly projecting and recoiling off-white metal letters fill the spaces between the beams, creating the impression of a structure in which the body of the letters and the beams support each other: huge building blocks made of beams and words.

On the ground floor, the letters *RBC*, each measuring almost 3 meters, identify the building, and a large *M* its location (Montpellier). The words found in the upper stories do not name the types or brands of furniture on display, but instead the activities related to their purchase: cooking, eating, lighting, storing, living—as well as atmospheres and moods, such as *seeing*, *dreaming*, *creating*.

The building plays with the elements of department store architecture and advertising, of classical tectonics, and of late-modern technicism. It thus becomes a complex collage aiming to entice visitors to purchase the merchandise on show.

RANGER
RBC
VOIR

The view from the street onto the RBC Design Center is unconventional. Nouvel grants the observer a view into the interior, with its eight split levels.

The protruding and recessed, three-dimensional letters are slotted into the grooves in the facade. The main sign stands on the ground and is the same height as the ground floor.

The two side facades are designed as display or advertising facades. The white words mounted on them are clearly visible from passing cars.

Project 22

GALERIES LAFAYETTE BERLIN DE / 1996

Architecture **JEAN NOUVEL, EMMANUEL CATTANI & ASSOCIÉS (PARIS FR)**

Typography **JEAN NOUVEL, EMMANUEL CATTANI & ASSOCIÉS**

The Lafayette department store—also known as Quartier 207—is one of the few glass buildings erected in Berlin's inner city in the 1990s. This was only possible because the plot was purchased shortly after the fall of the Berlin Wall, and because new building design regulations had not yet come into force. Designed by Jean Nouvel, Emmanel Cattani & Associates, the building is located at the corner of Friedrichstrasse and Französische Strasse. The architects were commissioned to design a building so spectacular in this prominent location that passersby would virtually be compelled to enter. Its interior and exterior merge at pavement level, permitting anyone to enter the store—and to be enraptured—exactly as intended by the architects.

The facade of what at first seems a calm and enclosed building volume is semitransparent and affords—depending on the lighting atmosphere and inside lighting—a view of the store's complex interior. Nouvel has integrated two historical elements of characteristic department store typology: he has rhythmically divided the dark facade using surrounding beams, a design that clearly accentuates the building's various stories, and his interior refers to the famous *coupoles* of the Parisian parent store. The cupolas have been formed into two cones, one extending from the ground floor into the upper stories, the other tapering off upward, piercing the roof and becoming a sky dome. This motif is repeated by another fifteen smaller cones standing upside down. Spanning three to five stories, these inverted cones pervade the building from the top down, flooding it with light and structuring the retail spaces.

Large-scale, multistory shopping palaces began to edge out smaller, single-story stores at the turn of the last century. One of the effects of this development was that lettering now climbed the facades from the ground floor upward. The large volumes were easily visible in urban space and were well suited to the affixing of advertising. Above-entrance signs and window lettering were extended by *fascias* (Italian for "band") enveloping the upper stories. Gold-leaf letters were applied onto glass mounted on the reverse side of these historical bands and covered with a second, black layer.

Nouvel took over and modernized this typology, enabling the illuminated letters on Berlin's Lafayette store to be clipped onto ribbon-shaped conductor rails. The building's name stands out emblazoned on its curvature. The letter/numbers Q 207 form a resplendent red neon sign and are distributed—like glowworms—across the facade.

On the outside, the Galeries Lafayette store exhibits a classic department store facade. The stories are marked by shiny bands running around the structure. The original plans had brand names integrated into these bands as illuminated signs.

Project 23

HACKNEY EMPIRE THEATRE LONDON GB / 2004

Architecture **TIM RONALDS ARCHITECTS (LONDON GB)**

Typography **RICHARD HOLLIS (LONDON GB)**

The Hackney Empire theater is situated in the center of the borough of Hackney, adjacent to the town hall. The Empire is one of the finest surviving variety theaters in Britain. Designed by Frank Matcham and opened in 1901, it has welcomed such performers as Charlie Chaplin, Stan Laurel, and Louis Armstrong.

Following an international competition, Tim Ronalds Architects undertook the restoration of the wonderful, listed 1,400-seat auditorium, and the construction of a new stage and backstage building as well as a new front-of-house building. The refurbishing project from 2001 to 2004 involved, among other things, building a new edifice on the prominent corner site of Mare Street and Wilton Way to provide front-of-house facilities.

Tim Ronalds Architects explored many ideas for the elevation of this building, seeking something that would coexist with the architecture of the historic theater and would have meaning for local people. The architects wanted a solution that was no less three-dimensional than the historic building, something that would be modern in spirit, and promote the theatre and its productions clearly.

As Tim Ronalds remarks, the idea of the giant lettering surfaced the way ideas do ... It seemed important to him that the lettering was part of the architecture, not an applied sign; hence the letters are massive and realized in the same material as the building itself. Tim Ronalds Architects wanted the lettering to look heavy but not have obvious support. The structural engineer, Philip Cooper, devised the "look no hands" structural solution.

In early drawings of models, the office used the font Letraset Compacta, which was an English design from the early 1960s. Tim Ronalds asked the well-known graphic designer and design historian Richard Hollis—who is a good friend—for his help in refining the typography. The font that Hollis chose for this task was adapted and redrawn from a newspaper advertising billboard and refers to theater posters from the beginning of the last century.

The letters were made of terra-cotta and concrete and hoisted onto their slender steel brackets. Although they look awfully heavy, they seem to *float* at the same time. This impression is supported by the fact that the letters *Y* and *E* emerge at the right side of the building.

The more than 3-meter-high letters are composed of cement cores clad in terra-cotta. In spite of their size and weight, they appear to float in front of the facade.

Project 24

USTER WORK CENTER USTER CH / 2009

Architecture **HODEL ARCHITEKTEN (WETZIKON CH)**

Typography **HI – VISUELLE GESTALTUNG (LUCERNE CH)**

Product design David Weisser, fokusform (Zurich CH)

With assisted accommodation for 120 and work and training facilities for 160, the Uster Work Center offers a wide range of possibilities for people with disabilities. The center is equipped with different kinds of workshops, including for screen printing, metalwork, and woodwork. And it was above all the theme of work that informed the concept by the designer duo commissioned to devise the signaletics for the remodeling and extension of the work center.

Megi Zumstein and Claudio Barandun engaged in a particular process. Together with the management of the center, they developed a concept for signage elements in the internal workshops based on the idea that the design should explicitly represent the technical and production options offered by the center. For the designers, the conceptual challenge lay in finding a balance between their aesthetic aspirations and an easy way for the center's workshop staff to produce the elements.

In close collaboration with the designers, the product designer David Weisser developed a modular system using as many uniform elements as possible and was responsible for their construction, interconnection, and installation. The segments of the large main signs in the exterior and interior areas are all cut at an angle of 67.5 degrees from the same squared timber as used for the other elements. These segments have been joined to form letters, numbers, and arrows, producing a slightly angular, typographic appearance. The basic symbols can be supplemented with square pieces of wood that can be arranged in series on threaded rods. All the elements are made of thermally treated wood (ash).

All signage elements were produced in the center's own workshops, screen-printed onsite, and mounted with the help of the Burkhardt carpentry firm from Wädenswil. The initial signage was produced under the supervision of the designers, and staff members have now taken over responsibility for improvements and adaptations themselves. The signage system has proved itself in the center's daily operations and is therefore both meaningful and attractive.

EMPFANG
WOHNHEIM

The signage is based on a modular system consisting of wooden elements that can be screen-printed and combined on threaded rods.

Using the system to create interior signage indicating the different stories.

All signage elements are manufactured in the workshops of this home for disabled people by the residents themselves.

The external signage is also made of wood, in this case ash. It is exposed to the weather and is changing color as the years pass.

Project 25

COTTBUS LIBRARY COTTBUS DE / 2004

Architecture **HERZOG & DE MEURON (BASEL CH)**
Typography **HERZOG & DE MEURON**

Jacques Herzog and Pierre de Meuron conceived the Cottbus Library as a stand-alone structure. As a landmark, it self-confidently projects the spirit of the young university; at the same time, the building—among other reasons, due to its conspicuous biomorphic form—connects with its surroundings in manifold ways. The architects emphasize that the structure was derived from an analysis of different sequences of movement within the building while also referring to the image of an amoeba. These unicellular organisms do not have a fixed form but change their shape constantly by forming pseudopodia (plasma appendages) that enable them to move. The image is a fitting one because the appearance of the building also changes under different light conditions and according to which side one approaches it from. At first glance the building seems closed to its surroundings; its multiple levels, for instance, are not discernible by day and only become visible when the building is illuminated at night. The entrance is located in a cleft cut into the smooth, rounded skin, and although reduced to a minimum, is still distinctive.

The glass facade has been printed on both sides with a typographic ornament that recalls the irregular grid of letters printed on the inside of banking envelopes designed to prevent the contents from being discerned through scanning. The effect of this pattern, which comprises several superimposed layers of different texts, languages, alphabets, and fonts, is simultaneously to homogenize and dissolve the structure on several levels. The pattern breaks up the reflection from the glass, softens the harsh impression created by the material, and thereby supports the flowing-closed softness of the structural form. The letters have been rendered illegible. They are detached from the text lines and starkly abstracted. Reduced to their pictorial expressiveness, they adapt to the architecture while at the same time, as an all-over, to some extent dissolving its tectonics.

Even though there is nothing concrete to be read, the facade refers to the interior of the building, subtly commenting on its use as a library. Through the interweaving of diverse linguistic elements, the curtain wall becomes a kind of meta-text that points to the immense knowledge stored in libraries and serving the accumulation of human knowledge. Whereas linguistic confusion prevented the completion of the Tower of Babel, here it becomes an actually built expression of a globalized knowledge society.

The glass panels have been screen-printed with a white pattern comprising different superimposed layers of texts, languages, alphabets, and fonts.

The effect of the curtain wall is to both homogenize and dissolve the building. A view to the outside through the layer of lettering.

The letters are detached from the text lines and starkly abstracted. By reducing them to their pictorial expressiveness, the designers have adapted them to the architecture.

Project 26

BEST ANTI-SIGN BUILDING RICHMOND USA / 1978

Architecture **SITE ARCHITECTURE (NEW YORK USA)**

Typography **SITE ARCHITECTURE**

The so-called Anti-Sign Project breaks ranks with the legendary series of buildings designed between 1972 and 1979 by SITE architects for the retail chain BEST Products. For the Peeling, Tilt, and Notch Buildings, the architects formulated the facades in spectacular material and spatial terms (inspired by medieval false facades) [see p. 65]. These buildings themselves became signs and thus rendered lettering proper obsolete—unlike the Anti-Sign Project, where the lettering *BEST* occupies two entire facades, each 10 meters high and 120 meters long.

The gray letters on the lettering band gradually dissolve, overlapping and thickening, to become a typographical ornament. This design—as James Wines explains—was by no means voluntary, but instead resulted from an unforeseen problem: half of the plot lay in the District of Richmond, the other half in the District of Virginia. The varying building regulations current at the time in the two districts meant that the company logo could measure 9 meters on one side but only 2 meters on the other!

Determined to have building-size letters on all facades, the SITE architects proposed lettering legible only on half of the facade while for the other half they created an illegible wall graphic from the overlapping letters. The building authority responsible for the illegible half classified this graphic image as abstract art and hence as approvable. The lesson being that designers may regard statutory requirements as a restriction, but also as a challenge! Their clever idea helped the SITE architects not only to resolve a practical problem but also to create added design value.

With the blessing of the art-loving company owners, SITE defamiliarized the BEST logo. Quite astonishingly, this convincing handling of corporate design elements on architectural structures found few imitators. In the age of dynamic logos, such solutions no longer represent anti-design in the strict sense …

The 9-meter-high, anthracite-colored letters cover two facades. To the left, the word *BEST* is clearly legible, while to the right, the letters increasingly overlap.

Project 27

THE NEW SCHOOL NEW YORK USA / 2014

Architecture **SOM ARCHITECTURE (NEW YORK USA)**

Graphic design **INTÉGRAL RUEDI BAUR (PARIS FR)**

Clad in hand-finished brass shingles, the building designed by the renowned architectural firm of Skidmore, Owen and Merill that stands on the corner of 5th Avenue and 14th Street in Manhattan has one particular feature that informed the design of the three-dimensional main signage and the orientation elements inside the building. Conspicuous on the otherwise orthogonally aligned sixteen-floor building are the angled, glazed access corridors, which are tectonically formed toward the inside, as if pressed into the facade. These interior streets form a variety of meeting and relaxation areas and are clearly readable from the outside.

The fact that the font family used should be comprehensive and have a three-dimensional effect was clear at an early stage based on an analysis of the architecture. However, the question still needed to be answered as to which font was best suited to this task. After several tests, the designers selected Peter Bilak's Irma font as the basis for their designs. They created fourteen variants that cast different degrees of shadow and allowed for a high degree of variability in the way they were used. The higher one goes in the building, the bolder the lettering becomes—as if aiming to help people maintain contact with the ground.

The main lettering was already positioned in the red-clad access area on the first floor in a sketch for SOM's competition submission. However, the idea of making it three-dimensional was only formulated after the development of the font family. The designer David Thoumazeaux—one of three product/industrial designers at intégral Ruedi Baur—created the structurally complex typeface based on sketches by Ruedi Baur. It moves in different directions, not only diminishing toward the tapered front but also becoming smaller along the lateral edge. In addition, the letterforms project in different directions and their surfaces exhibit different inclinations. Only the baseline of the white script remains constant. In combination with the red color, which enables the letters to optically fuse with the wall behind them, this ensures a visual stability within the overall dynamism.

It goes without saying that the task of finding a craftsman who could translate this lettering design into reality was not easy. The letters were constructed by an American metalworker, who also installed the lighting technology inside them. The illumination concept is also a sophisticated one. The letter bodies are open to the front and translucent Plexiglas plates have been installed in them at a depth of around 5 centimeters. These provide for an even distribution of the light emitted by LEDs at the back of the letters. The possibility of mundane, primarily informative signage verging on art can never be excluded. Just ask James Turrell.

Baur confronts an inward folding of the facade with an interior protuberance—a communicatively succinct counter-gesture. However, he does so without perforating the facade. He takes into account the strict signaletics prescriptions in Manhattan and at the same time shows how to make maximum use of them. It is an impressive feat.

The three-dimensional lettering is mounted on the red-painted back wall of the corridor on the first floor.

In tectonic terms, the letters are highly complex and—although this is not obvious at first glance—open at the front. The illuminating elements inside them are set back several centimeters.

The access corridors are positioned at the front of the building and about the facade. The main signage has, as it were, been shifted from the exterior to the interior.

The three-dimensional font family was derived from the angled, inwardly formed access zones.

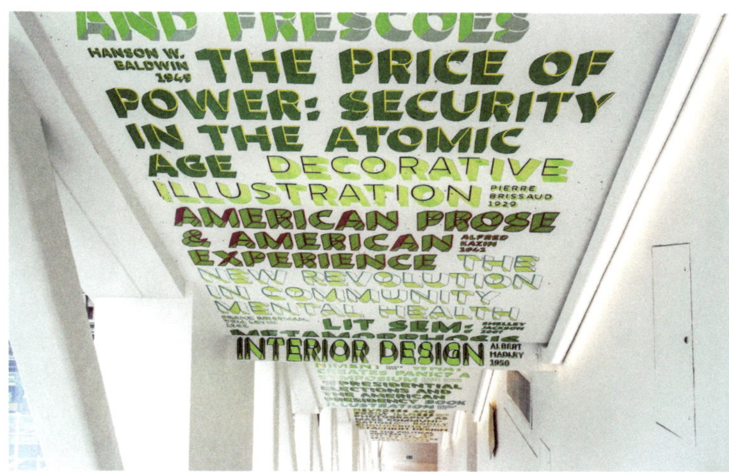

Project 28

DORFLINDE NURSING HOME ZURICH CH / 2011

Architecture **NEFF NEUMANN ARCHITEKTEN AG (ZURICH CH)**

Typography **HI – VISUELLE GESTALTUNG (LUCERNE CH)**

Today, the old linden tree that once marked the center of the village of Oerlikon[1] outside Zurich is still standing—healthy and magnificent—near this typical 1970s development. The newer buildings were arranged around the village linden, thus giving the area its name.

In 1972 the artist Franz Grossert installed a highly abstract representation of a linden tree in the middle of the nursing home's reception area, thereby symbolically duplicating the real one. He made the trunk out of pieces of colored ceramic and the overhanging foliage from geometric pieces of wood of different thicknesses, the horizontal surfaces of which are painted light yellow and the edges burgundy. Apart from this expressive sculpture, the building also features an unusually large number of other striking artworks.

The decision by the architects Barbara Neff and Bettina Neumann to place art at the center of their remodeling and renovation project brought success. The aim of the project was not only to combine the old and the new as seamlessly as possible; the designers were also explicitly concerned with giving the existing art from the 1970s more space, to give it a stage on which its effect could fully unfold. This approach was supported by Vreni Spieser's contemporary intervention. Her ceiling-high wallpapers printed with color progressions create a specific color atmosphere on each floor, which—as a secondary effect—helps the residents orient themselves within the building.

The Lucerne studio Atelier Hi – Visuelle Gestaltung has made a name for itself with different signage projects that reference the history, formal characteristics, or materials of buildings. Megi Zumstein and Claudio Barandun always look for themes in buildings that can inform exterior and interior signage design, and have developed a keen sense for what can work.

In the case of the Dorflinde nursing home, Grossert's expressive sculpture offered a starting point for their designs. It initially took them in two directions, leading to one variant made of ceramics and one made of three-dimensionally formed plates. Both solutions could have been effectively integrated into the architecture. However, the second option was more idiosyncratic, fitted in optimally with the architecture, and was also more cost-effective.

What is special about the Dorflinde project is that the signaletics were derived from a historical building-art project, the formal qualities of which were transferred to and updated in the signage objects. The latter fulfill an explicitly communicative task and—together with the sculpture and other artworks—strengthen the identity of the building.

1 Oerlikon was incorporated into Zurich in 1934.

The individual letters are constructed from layered material of different heights and painted in the same colors as the sculpture.

The signage was derived from the expressive ceiling elements that form part of the construction art project by Franz Grossert, undertaken in 1972. The work is an abstract representation of a linden tree and refers to the name of the nursing home.

Part 3

APPENDIX

THE CHANGE IN SIGNAGE TYPES

Precursors of contemporary building signage
Many of the signage types we are familiar with today already existed in antiquity: inscriptions, painted signs, and plaques. Carved lettering on temples and architraves was often of a religious nature. This technique was later used in secular contexts, that is, for everyday buildings. Plaques made of terra-cotta and stone were the forerunners of signs made of iron, wood, ceramic, and glass used by medieval taverns, shops, and guilds. Carved, jointed, painted, and hung characters on public and private buildings—including livestock buildings, barns, etc.—communicated the name of the owner, the date of construction, the trade, or the location.

A small proportion of labeled buildings
In contrast to villages and cities, houses exhibited names only when they constituted important landmarks that served orientation. "As a rule not every building is proprially[1] designated, only the most well-known, attractive and interesting among them (...)."[2] Signage was installed on public buildings such as inns, hospitals, hotels, and administrative institutions.

Words and pictures
Both so-called "speaking" signs, which featured images[3] or emblems,[4] and "non-speaking" signs, which featured mythological and religious symbols, could be deciphered by the majority of the population. As literacy levels increased over the centuries, pictorial signs—in some cases painted by famous artists such as Antoine Watteau and Gustave Courbet—were supplemented with explanatory texts or completely replaced by worded signs.[5]

More competition, more advertising
The terms *Schild*[6] (sign) and *Tafel*[7] (plaque), which are still commonly used in the German-speaking world, date from the emergence of the craft and service guilds in the Middle Ages. Guild emblems expressed membership of a particular professional group. As long as the obligation to join a guild remained in force, no further advertising measures were required; a sign—for example, one bearing the guild's emblem—sufficed as an indication of the trade carried out in the respective building. The decline of mandatory guild membership led to an increase in run on competition between market participants and the commercial forms of advertising we are familiar with today: fliers, posters, newspaper advertising. Shops, factories, and headquarters now began to display not only the names of owners and operators but also large and conspicuous brand logos and advertising posters.

The change in signage techniques
Classical, integral signage such as inscriptions carved in stone, sgraffiti, and inlays made of different materials in roofs, floors, and facades exists in many variants. Over time these abrasive[8] techniques were supplemented or replaced altogether by "installable" signage forms such as signs, billboards, and individual letters. Whereas signs were once manufactured from wood or metal, today they are predominantly made of synthetic materials. Easily exchangeable advertising banners and megaposters are replacing painted advertising on firewalls and facades (wood, masonry, and plastered walls).[9]

Letters made of metal, wood, ceramic, and so on are mounted individually with bolts on facades, in some cases with a space between the characters and the supporting surface. These letters can be prefabricated in the workshop. Signage formed from individual letters does not conceal the facade, unlike planar signs and casings, which for this reason are no longer approved in many places.

Today, signage on smooth surfaces, in particular on glass, is for the most part cut from plastic film. Since the last quarter of the twentieth century, large-scale screen printing has been possible, in some cases on site. Using this technique, glass facades, for example, can be printed with translucent lettering and typo-ornaments, which produces a similar impression to the older technique of acid etching. In recent years, screen printing has been replaced by digital direct printing processes, in which the colors are hardened with UV light.

These signage techniques are supplemented by methods in which the surface structure is transformed by chemical-thermal processes, such as anodization and black-finishing. Currently, experiments are being conducted with 3D printing processes, with which letters and casting molds will be printed in the future.

Non-illuminated signage types have an effect by day but are illegible by night. Whereas signs were illuminated in the Middle Ages using torches, this is done today with floodlights and spotlights.

Signage composed of points of light
While new signage techniques continually changed townscapes, fundamental change first came with the invention of the lightbulb in the middle of the nineteenth century. This new lighting technique replaced the gas

lanterns that had hitherto been the basic form of lighting in cities and made the first illuminated signage possible. The first illuminated letters were formed from points of light emitted by lightbulbs. Soon it became possible to electrically control flashing sequences to suggest movement. In 1867 the poet Julius Rodenberg already remarked:

"Soon there is twinkling and flashing everywhere. All of Paris is sown with golden points (...), lines form from the points, the lines become figures, and endless alleys of light are visible as far as the eye can see."[10]

At the Berlin hygiene exhibition in 1883, the word EDISON was illuminated in alternating letters.[11] These intermittently flashing signs were the forerunners of today's digital screens and media facades, which radiate moving letters and images and, in addition—and this is a new element—facilitate a rapid updating of information.

Neon lettering and symbols

Georges Claude presented his moldable glass tubes filled with neon gas for the first time at the Paris Transport Fair in 1910. While introduced all over the world, they proved particularly popular in the USA between 1920 and 1960. The first neon installations on Broadway and in Times Square in New York, many of them designed by Douglas Leigh, became popular tourist attractions.

Approaching the new medium of light

In a 1927 essay entitled *Lichtreklame und Architektur* ("Illuminated Advertising and Architecture"), the German architect and architectural theorist Hugo Häring criticized the fact that the (German) city by night still presented a "carnival-like chaos of diverse illuminated advertisements."[12] In an essay from 1928,[13] Ernst May, who was Frankfurt am Main's municipal architect between 1925 and 1930, stated that the groundbreaking American developments in the field of advertising needed to be "channeled properly in design terms" to ensure that they conformed to the idea of order promulgated by the Neues Bauen (New Building) movement. In contrast to the large, colorful neon advertisements that were spread carelessly across American facades—and regarded by some in Europe as kitsch and offensive—such illumination, in May's view, needed to become an integral part of the architecture.

Erich Mendelsohn's trip to New York in 1926 inspired him to create an integral lighting architecture. He created his groundbreaking designs with their effect by night and the dynamics of street traffic in mind, introducing horizontal bands of light and integrating illuminated signage into upper floors or positioning it on projecting structures.

Illuminated advertising becomes a lucrative business

Following the First World War, the interest of municipal authorities in the revenue that could be gained from advertisers led to the breakthrough of illuminated signs in Europe. Power companies began to increase the supply of electrical current. In 1928, the shared interests of municipal authorities and industry led to a "lighting campaign" in Germany. Berlin businesses proposed that the possibilities offered by the new medium could be explored during a "propaganda week" in which cultural institutions, designers, and municipal planning and building offices could all take an active part. The campaign was launched with the exhibition *Berlin im Licht* ("Berlin in the Light") in autumn 1928. The goal was to cultivate a broader acceptance of electric lighting among the population and to demonstrate its many possible applications. In Zurich, a "lighting week" also took place in 1932 to better acquaint the population with the "applications of electric light." A competition was held calling for lighting designs for squares, buildings, and residential streets. Numerous prominent Swiss designers took part, including Max Bill and Alfred Willimann, as well as the photographer Hans Finsler.

Political propaganda

During the 1930s, the Italian fascists and the German National Socialists used neon-lit advertising for propaganda purposes. During the Second World War that followed, illuminated advertising was affected by compulsory blackouts and the lack of electricity, and the production of illuminated signage came to an almost complete standstill. During the electricity blockade in 1948–49, Berlin, for example, was largely in darkness. The establishment of an independent electricity supply enabled West Berlin to illuminate itself again, and Kurfürstendamm, for example, once again became the shining boulevard by night that it had been before the war.

The *Berlin soll leuchten!* ("Berlin should shine") campaign in 1957 symbolized the economic rise of West Berlin and aimed to emphasize the contrast with the Eastern bloc countries. During the Cold War, (state-decreed) illuminated advertising was used in countries such as Poland[14] and East Germany[15] to suggest the idea of a functioning economy to the local population and the rest of the world.

Let there be neon!

In the 1950s, neon fever broke out again in Europe. Bold neon signage in the fonts typical of this period (such as the Mistral font designed by Robert Escoffon in 1953) drew people into newly constructed cinemas, department stores, shops, and restaurants. These signs represented economic progress and provided a touch of glamour in war-damaged but now quickly growing cities and tourist destinations. In some places, particularly in nightclub districts such as St. Pauli in Hamburg, the Pigalle quarter in Paris, and London's West End, colorful neon advertising covered entire buildings.

Las Vegas, a city devoted to leisure and gambling, which was founded in the middle of the Nevada desert in 1905, developed into a neon mecca. Las Vegas is known for its casinos with their large adjoining hotel complexes. The first giant neon advertising structures were installed on the facades of casinos such as the Horseshoe and the Stardust. The American multimedia artist Rudi Stern[16] characterizes the city as follows: Las Vegas sells the American Dream (...) If form and function are meant to be related, then Las Vegas seems an excellent example (...) Las Vegas is an electric phantasy meant to sell itself, and neon and electric architecture here are clearly "on premise" advertising.

Many renowned neon designers and specialist firms such as the Young Electric Sign Company contributed to this bizarre total work of art. At the industry's high point, around 1940, almost two thousand larger and smaller companies were producing neon signs. The industry began to decline in the 1960s. Neon tubes were now concealed in closed lettering with translucent coverings or clad in light boxes. However, the neon tube has never really disappeared and is still used, above all by artists such as Bruce Nauman and Dan Flavin. Today, collectors and museums search for old, famous neon signage, disassembling and meticulously restoring it before putting it on display.[17]

The transformation of the illuminated sign market in the postwar period

Self-illuminating letter casings covered with colored acrylic glass or exhibiting letters cut from adhesive film began to replace exposed neon tubes in the 1950s, and these offered a significantly more striking form of advertising. However, they also used a large amount of electricity and interfered with facade designs and roof silhouettes due to their sometimes solid supporting structures. Since the 1990s, longer-life and more environmentally friendly LEDs have been replacing neon tubes. Specialist firms and facade constructors now use them to realize large LED walls and media facades.

The postwar period saw the creation of large signage firms that still serve the mass market today, creating series of illuminated signs for international concerns and installing them in buildings nationally or worldwide. Most European signage firms are now facing serious competition from Asian producers, which are manufacturing different elements (LEDs and injection-molded lettering) at a much lower price than European firms.

New impulses

Recently, thinking in the illuminated signage sector has been tending more in the direction of qualitative (integral) projects. New possibilities are being explored, particularly in the context of smaller and medium-sized projects. Manufacturers are again working more directly with the new generation of architects and graphic designers, contributing the extensive knowledge they have accumulated over many years. Experimentation with materials, construction forms, lighting technology, and spaces by architects, designers, and production firms is constantly producing new types of signage. Old techniques are being refined and new needs adapted to.

Handmade

Of late, there has also been a renaissance of high-quality handmade exterior advertising. In the USA, signage on small shops is again being produced by hand,[18] and global enterprises are using customized handmade signage techniques to differentiate themselves from their competitors.

The following chapter offers an overview of the different techniques involved in signage production.

1 i. e., with a proper name
2 Wolodymyr Kamianets, "Zur Einteilung der deutschen Eigennamen," *Grazer Linguistische Studien* 54 (2000).
3 e. g., a barber cutting hair
4 e. g., a pretzel indicates a bakery; the precursor of today's pictograms
5 See Alla Powlichina and Jewgeni Kowtun, *Das russische Reklameschild und die Künstler der Avantgarde* (Leningrad: Aurora Kunstverlag, 1991).
6 From Middle High German *schilt*, "war shield" (often decorated with painted emblems); Engl. "guild."
7 From Middle High German *tafel*, a board or something similar in guildhalls exhibiting the guild symbols; Engl. "guild sign."
8 From the Latin *abradere*, "to scrape off."
9 In recent years a number of works have been published on the phenomenon of disappearing facade paintings or "ghost signs." See, for example, *Cynthia Lea Haas, Ghost Signs of Arkansas (Fayetteville: University of Arkansas Press, 1997).*
10 Cited from FVL, Fachverband für Lichtwerbung e.V., *Signaturen der Nacht – Die Welt der Lichtwerbung* (Ludwigsburg: avedition GmbH, 2009).
11 The invention of the constantly illuminating light bulb is attributed to Thomas Alva Edison.
12 Typescript of a lecture given at the 16th annual meeting of the Deutsche Beleuchtungstechnische Gesellschaft, held in Karlsruhe on June 22, 1928.
13 Ernst May, "Städtebau und Lichtreklame," in *Licht und Beleuchtung*, ed. Wilhelm Lotz (Berlin: Verlag Hermann Reckendorf, 1928).
14 Ilona Karwinska, *Polish Cold War Neon* (New York: Mark Batty, 2009).
15 *Plaste und Elaste – Leuchtreklame in der DDR* (Berlin: Neues Leben Verlag, 2010).
16 Rudi Stern, *Let There Be Neon* (Cincinnati: ST Publications, 1979).
17 Neon Museum Las Vegas *(www.neonmuseum.org)*; Buchstabenmuseum Berlin (www.buchstabenmuseum.de).
18 www.signpaintersfilm.com

ANATOMY OF LETTERING

majuscules
= upper case letters
minuscules
= lower case letters
serif typeface / serif
= letters with "feet"
grotesque / sans serif
= letters without "feet"

1 apex
2 downstroke
3 bowl
4 shoulder
5 hook
6 bar
7 dot / tittle
8 arm
9 eye / counter
10 upstroke
11 crossbar
12 stem / vertical stroke
13 leg
14 serif
15 spur
16 ligature
17 body size / body height
18 cap height / H height
19 ascender line
20 x-height
21 baseline
22 descender line

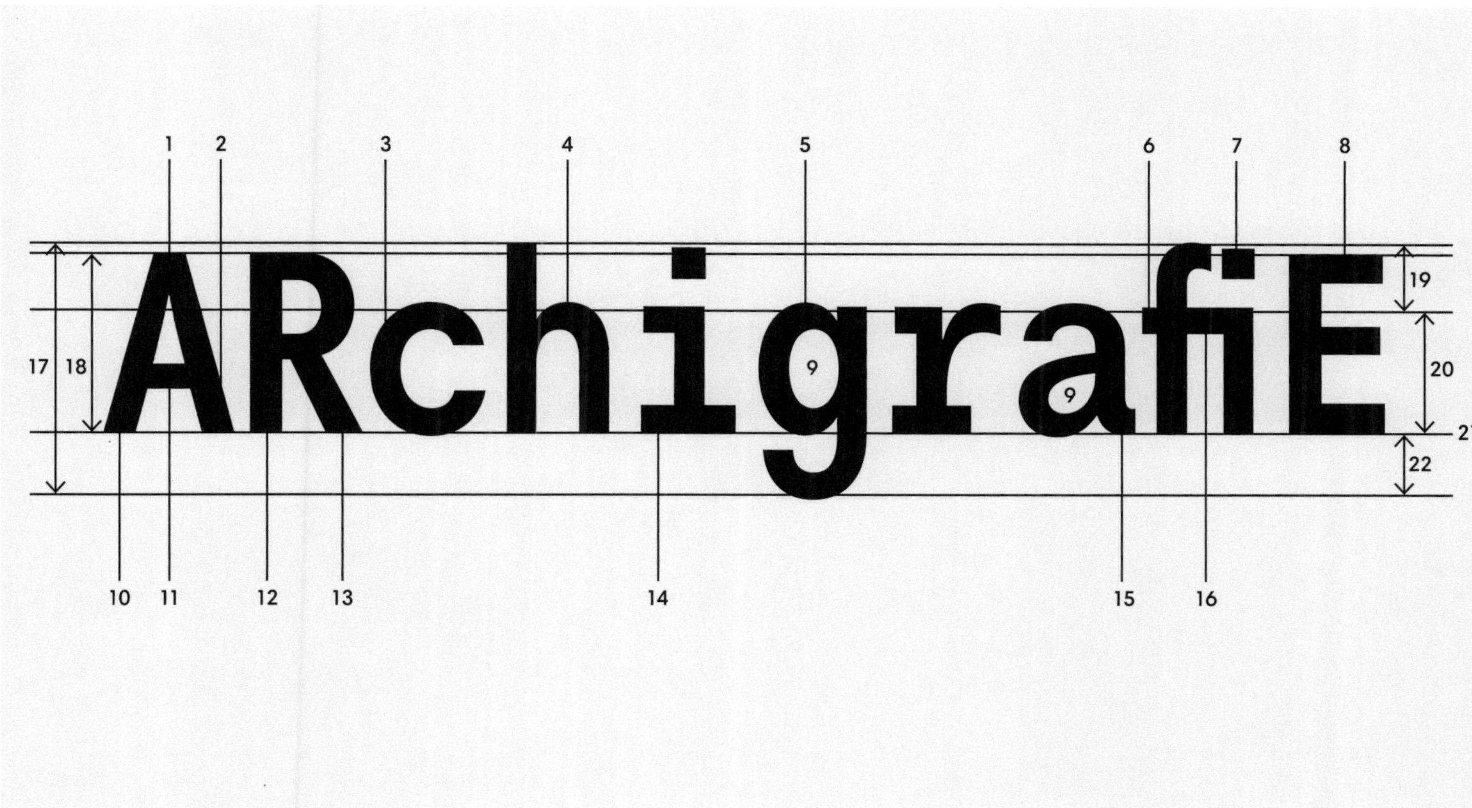

SPATIAL GRAPHICS—
GRAPHICS IN SPACE

Designing and constructing signage requires a great deal of technical know-how and is much more than a classic graphic design task. How can letters be spatially shaped, given material form, and constructed? What color systems exist in the building industry? How are particular lighting effects achieved? There are few limits to the technical possibilities and ways of experimenting with materials and construction methods. This chapter presents an overview of different signage techniques and attempts to classify them. The boundaries between the types of techniques are fluid and often several are combined.

1. Abrasive processes
Creating signage by partially removing surface material is possible in the case of nearly all substrate materials. However, there are different ways in which this can be dome. Abrasive processes are suited above all to buildings used for the same purpose over the long term. Lettering is written directly into the building envelope; the facade is, as it were, "tattooed."

2. Equivalence/mutation processes
Small, manageable-sized modules such as bricks, roof tiles, and ceramic plates can be prefabricated in large numbers and are easy to work with. They are repetitively joined to walls and facades or mounted on roofs. Ornaments or lettering are created by selectively interweaving elements that are distinct from their surroundings in terms of color or space. Patination and chemical-electrical processes can also be used to change the surface effect without having to remove or add material.

3. Additive processes
Signage is usually installed on preexisting buildings. A number of signage techniques, such as painting, screen printing, and adhesive film, require the architecture as a supporting base and are implemented on site. Letters and signs made of materials such as wood, glass, or metal can be manufactured independently of the architecture and mounted following production. Signage that is applied to surfaces can be removed or painted over but usually leaves traces.

4. Self-illuminating signage
Illuminated signs make up a large part of the market, can be constructed in many ways, and require particular (light-) technical know-how.

5. Animated signage types
Bringing life to signage through animation and covering entire facades with up-to-date information and moving images was a dream that drove many designers at the beginning of the twentieth century [see p. 14]. Today, these fantasies are in part coming true with the aid of new technologies. The development of digital screens and media facades means that content no longer needs to be fixed as in the case of conventional, analog signage. If the number of such screens is to be kept under control, ways for advertisers, artists, and government authorities to share these facilities will need to be explored.

Due to the impact they have on public space, the installation of such facilities is usually subject to special approval procedures by the relevant municipal authorities, with a particular emphasis on traffic safety.

1.1

INSCRIPTIONS: CHISELING

Chiseling inscriptions is one of the oldest signage techniques. The letters are hewn out of the stone—mostly in the form of wedge-shaped indentations—with a chisel. The types of chisel or punch used vary according to the hardness of the stone and the desired lettering. Such indentations can be painted or gilded to improve legibility. As an alternative to this "negative" method, letters can also be recessed-raised or free-standing raised. In such cases the material around the lettering is chiseled away. Today, stone inscriptions are not often made because they cannot be altered. Moreover, they are expensive due to the enormous amount of work required by the stonemason or sculptor even with the help of pneumatic tools.

1.2

INSCRIPTIONS: MILLING / ENGRAVING

Facade materials such as metal, wood, concrete, and plastic can be worked with CNC[1] milling machines. This technique allows for the unproblematic creation of negative and positive reliefs as well as small and very precise lettering, logos, and ornaments.

1.3

INSCRIPTIONS: BLASTING

Because quartz sand was formerly used as a blasting material, the term "sandblasting" is still more commonly used than "compressed air blasting." Glass, wood, concrete, or metal are sprayed with an abrasive material—sand, glass, corundum, aluminum, or chromium oxide—under pressure. Differences in the grain size of the abrasive material result in different matte, rough, and fine surface structures. The motif is applied to the substrate using plotted film or screen printing. This layer covers the area that is not to be blasted.

Motifs blasted onto glass have a very special quality. They appear matte yet absorb the surrounding color and react to changing light conditions over the course of the day. In rainy conditions the blasted areas become almost completely transparent, and pictures and letters seem to partly dissolve.

1 computerized numerical control

1.4

INSCRIPTIONS: SCRATCHING / SGRAFFITO

In the case of the sgraffito technique,[2] ornaments and letters are scored or scratched "al fresco,"[3] i.e., into layers of plaster that have not yet hardened. To ensure that there is a clear contrast between texts/drawings and the plaster, different colors are used for the base plaster and the final rendering.

2 The term *sgraffito* (or scraffito) is derived from the Italian verb *sgraffiare*, "to scratch."

3 Italian: "in the open air"

1.5

ETCHING

Different etching agents and techniques are used depending on the material to be written on. Sections that are not supposed to be recessed and matted are protected in advance with a masking lacquer—also known as an etching ground. In the case of relief engraving the motif is protected using masking lacquer, whereas in the case of deep etching it is the area around the motif that is covered.

Glass is etched with hydrofluoric acid. Different durations of application produce different degrees of matting. The surface structure is finer and more brilliant than that produced by compressed air blasting. Etched glass is easy to clean and is almost scratch-proof.

Concrete elements can be worked in a similar way. A film is screen-printed with setting retarder and laid in the concrete formwork. The setting of the concrete is retarded on the sections that are to be printed. The text or pictorial motif can be brushed free after the removal of the formwork.

Conductive metals are etched electrolytically. A stencil is laid on the area that is to be inscribed and an electrolytic paste is applied before the metal is connected to an electricity source. The parts that are not covered are etched into the surface of the metal. Following this (inscription) process, the metal piece is treated with a neutralizer.

Etching techniques are not completely unproblematic. Many agents can be harmful to health and need to be handled in accordance with the relevant safety measures. Etching agents must be disposed of correctly.

2.1

ASSEMBLING: MODULAR / FLAT

Creating signs on roofs by means of differently colored tiles is one of the oldest modular signage forms. This method has been used to display the year in which farms were established and the names of factories. The same effect can be achieved using different bricks or clinkers, or indeed any modularly joinable material (ceramic, cement asbestos, wood, or metal elements) on facades. Such signage anticipates, as it were, the digital principle. Each element forms a physical pixel and the smaller the individual elements and the more closely they are positioned together, the more precisely the signage is defined.

2.2

ASSEMBLING: MODULAR / THREE-DIMENSIONAL

Lettering and ornaments can also be created using spatial differences, i.e., by setting individual modules forward, recessing them, or positioning them at an angle. The basic form of bricks used in exposed masonry can also be varied. Many material-in-material solutions have a subtle, restrained appearance and for this reason are sometimes additionally emphasized with paint.

2.3

OXIDATION

Oxidation is a chemical reaction in which the number of electrons in a material is altered. In this process no protective layer is deposited on the material, unlike in galvanic coating processes. The uppermost layer of a metal is chemically transformed and thereby optically altered. There are different oxidation processes: aluminum is electrolytically oxidized (anodization); iron is black-finished by treating it with alkaline solutions. Natural oxidation can also be used for signage purposes. In this case, the material is protected from the aging process by a special transparent coating.

3.1

PAINTING: SIGN PAINTING

One of the oldest and simplest signage techniques involves painting directly onto facades. It is important to be well acquainted with the substrate, that is, the facade structure and material, in order to select the appropriate weather-resistant and long-wearing paint. Special—for example, luminescent or reflective—agents can be mixed with the pigment.

The way the paint is applied is also decisive. The dynamic characteristics of brush painting clearly distinguish it from the airbrush technique. Motifs are painted freehand onto the substrate or are applied using self-adhesive, negative stencils. In the first stage, the facade paint is applied to prevent the actual signage paint— which is applied in the second stage—from running under the stencil film.

3.2

PAINTING: REVERSE GLASS PAINTING / REVERSE GLASS METAL ETCHING

From the middle of the nineteenth century onward, reverse glass painting and reverse glass metal etching were used for signage on shops. In reverse glass painting, company names and advertising content are painted in reverse with an opaque paint on the inner side of panes of glass and then covered with a second color, e.g., black, to increase contrast. In the case of reverse glass metal etching, the paint is replaced by a metal film, such as gold, silver, brass, or aluminum leaf. Glass signs painted in this way were mounted flat or at a slight angle above display windows or entrances and in some cases structurally integrated. When the first large department stores were built at the end of the nineteenth and beginning of the twentieth century, architects also positioned bands of lettering on the upper sections of the facades. [p. 12].

3.3

PAINTING: SCREEN PRINTING, DIGITAL UV DIRECT PRINTING

Smooth facade materials such as sheet metal, glass, fiber cement, and polycarbonate are printed on in various ways and delivered to building sites as prefabricated elements.

Screen printing is a so-called porous printing process; screen frames are available in sizes up to 4 by 8 square meters[4] for use in the building industry. In the first step, the screen is completely exposed to light. The synthetic fabric is made ink-permeable with UV light where the motif is supposed to appear. The screen is then placed on the surface that is to be printed and the ink is pressed through the fabric with a squeegee. In the case of glass, ceramic screen printing can also be used. Here, the motif is burned in during the hardening of float glass to produce tempered glass at a temperature of 650°C. Glass marked in this way is extremely color stable and weather resistant—both important factors for use in outside areas.

As in reverse glass painting, glass printing is done on the back side of the pane. However, motifs can also be printed on the intermediate layers in insulating glass and laminated safety glass. This protects motifs not only from weather but above all from mechanical influences. In this case, two-component inks rather than ceramic inks are use.

3.4

GLUING: ADHESIVE FILM

Today, signage on smooth surfaces is usually created using weather- and UV-resistant plastic films. Manufacturers offer comprehensive color palettes as well as translucent and mirrored-effect films from which lettering can be cut based on digital templates. Films can be plotted, for example, with special colors, color gradients, and particular pictorial motifs. However, they are not UV resistant and must be laminated when used outside. Films can be glued on the inside of glass or, in the case of laminated safety glass, motifs can be printed directly onto the laminate film.

4 Germany 2016

3.5

CUTTING OUT: CUTOUT LETTERING

Letters, ornaments, and patterns can be cut out of all types of sheet materials and mounted on buildings. In the case of thinner materials they are milled or laser-cut. For thicker materials and stone, a water jet cutter is used. Using CNC technology, complex letters and patterns can be cut from a diverse range of materials at a relatively low cost, and such motifs have as a result proved very popular in recent years.

An important part of the design task involves devising a way to fix lettering to the substrate. Cutout letters can be mounted directly onto a facade or set out from it, which creates different shadow and perspectival effects. The way in which letters can be mounted depends on the properties and construction of the substrate. On solid facades (masonry, natural stone, cement) signage can be attached using embedded or glued-in threaded rods; reversible signage is attached using concealed screws. Drilling templates are used for precise mounting. Attaching letters to thin, back-ventilated facades and thermal insulation composite systems is a complex task, and the type of inserts to be used should be carefully discussed with the facade designers beforehand. When it comes to drilling into facades, it is important to know whether waterproofing can still be guaranteed.

3.6

CASTING

Letters can be cast out of materials such as metal, concrete, glass, or plastic, and special casting molds are manufactured for this purpose.

In concrete casting, wooden formwork is used with different surface structures. This formwork is cut slightly conically so that the cast product can be removed easily and without damaging it. Cast concrete lettering can be produced both on and off site and as positive or negative reliefs. In order to reduce the weight of larger concrete letters, polystyrene void formers are placed in the formwork and concealed by the poured concrete.

In most cases, the construction of the formwork is more expensive and time-consuming than the casting itself. Older, expensive casting processes for metal and glass using heat-resistant forms made of chamotte, ceramic, or sand are only rarely used today.

Today, lettering is also produced industrially using injection molding. Since the manufacture of injection molding tools is very expensive, this technique is only used for series of a thousand or more pieces. Only global enterprises with hundreds of branches require so many signs and can afford to pay for them.

In injection molding, synthetic granules are liquefied by heat and injected into a closed form under high pressure. After cooling and removal from the form, the resulting elements are galvanized or painted and assembled into logos or letters.

3.7

DEEP-DRAWN AND THERMOFORMED LETTERS

The technology involved in deep drawing is also expensive and thus only used for the production of fifty or more pieces. Wood or aluminum punches and dies are used in mechanical deep drawing, wood alone in vacuum deep drawing.

Originally, the letters produced by this process were made from thin metal plates, deep-drawn under high pressure. Today they are made from synthetics such as ABS.[5] polycarbonate, and acrylic glass, which are heated and then formed: thus the name "thermoforming."

In the case of vacuum deep drawing, plastic plates between 2 and 5 millimeters thick are drawn over the punch form in a vacuum. Motifs can be produced as positive or negative reliefs and up to a 150 by 280 centimeters.[6]

Acrylic glass plates can be screen-printed prior to the deep-drawing process, allowing for the reshaping of the material. To ensure that logos and letters are ultimately formed as desired, they are applied to the material in the form of digitally computed "wrong prints."

Logos and letters can also be sprayed, coated, or metallized with aluminum after the forming process. This metallization can be opaque or translucent, so that signage which appears metallic or reflective by day is illuminated by night. Deep-drawn letters made of ABS can also be electroplated, i.e., chromium plated, which is not possible in the case of acrylic glass.

5 Acrylonitrile butadiene styrene
6 Germany 2016

3.8

ASSEMBLED LETTERING

Large-scale lettering is assembled from individual sections by machine but also, in a surprising number of cases, by hand. In the case of the individual objects and small series commonly seen today, the edges are usually made of thermally formed acrylic glass while the back walls and fronts are composed of laser-cut acrylic glass plates. The individual elements are assembled into complete logos or letters, glued, and then varnished or coated with a film (in some cases printed beforehand).

3.9

PRINTING: 3-D PRINTING

3D printers can "print" three-dimensional letters by constructing successive layers of bonded synthetic powder (PMMA[7]) or molten filament (plastic wound around a spool like a wire). This technique is still at the pioneering stage but in the future will be used for the production of complex forms, individual objects, and small series. It will also be possible to 3D-print casting molds [see 3.6].

3.10

FACADE-MOUNTED SIGNAGE WITH LETTERING ON ONE SIDE

Formerly, signs were made of wood, glass, metal, or highly weather-resistant enamel but today are usually made of aluminum or plastic. As described above, a wide range of techniques are used to produce the lettering on these signs [see 3.1–3.4]. For reasons of stability, signs are often beveled or slightly curved. Different techniques are used to mount them flush with facades or slightly protruding from them at an angle.

7 Polymethyl methacrylate

3.11

PROJECTING SIGNS WITH LETTERING ON TWO OR MORE SIDES

Projecting signs—traditionally used on taverns and shops—are set at a right angle to the building facade. Often featuring handcrafted metalwork, they advertise businesses and trades not only with texts but also with graphic symbols and pictograms. The fact that they project out from the facade creates wind resistance, which necessitates solid anchoring. In narrow lanes in historic town centers it is required that these signs can be folded to the side to allow vehicles to pass unhindered.

3.12

PYLONS / STELES

Pylons are freestanding and structurally independent of a building. The category of pylon or column signage includes gigantic standard advertising steles offered by the advertising industry. Although these signage elements are dissociated from the architecture around them, they nevertheless interact with it as an additive element. In the best cases, they are coordinated with the architecture in terms of dimensions, construction, materials, and positioning. Installing steles requires the design of a suitable foundation.

3.13

SCULPTURAL LETTERING / LETTERING SCULPTURES

Lettering sculptures are particularly conspicuous and are relatively rare. In these “typotectures” the letters form part of the structure and are integrated into the construction or are completely formed in three dimensions and freestanding. It is possible to walk around these lettering sculptures, observing them from all sides. In the process, the two-dimensionality of writing clearly reveals itself through the difficulty of reading the letters in reverse from the back.

Due to the fact that it is easy to shape and to its static properties, concrete is particularly suitable for lettering sculptures, which can also be constructed of metal and wood.

4.1

SIGNAGE MADE OF POINT LIGHTS (FILAMENT LAMPS / LEDS)

The earliest self-illuminating signs were composed of individual, aligned filament lamps. The high power consumption of filament lamps led to their ban in the European Union in 2009. In recent years, LEDs[8] have become a standard technology due to their high energy efficiency.

The effectiveness of filament-lamp signage was increased early on by the use of sequential blinking. The first movement sequences were suggested using switching systems; later it became possible to display longer texts in the form of tickers. Filament-lamp signs represent the earliest form of moving media in public space.

Today, tickers consist of individually controllable LEDs mounted on plates in a grid-like pattern; these allow information to be updated at will. The transition to LED walls and entire media facades is ongoing.

8 light-emitting diodes

4.2

SIGNAGE MADE OF LINE LIGHTS (NEON SIGNS)

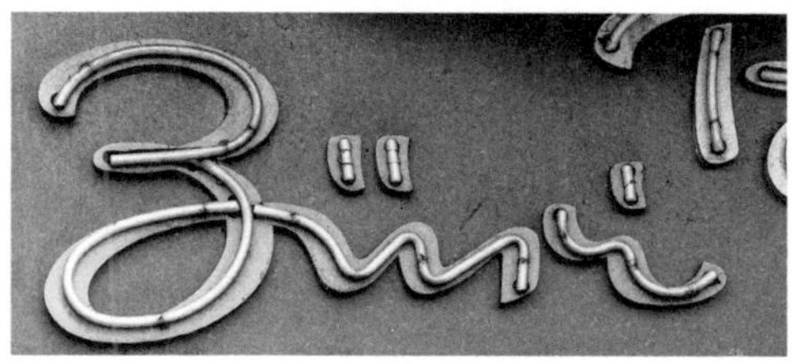

Neon lights are made by filling glass tubes with neon gas and ionizing it by applying a high charge to electrodes positioned at both ends of the tube. Pure neon emits a typically orange-red light. The addition of argon or mercury produces a blue light containing a high proportion of UV light. Coatings on the inside of the tube transform the UV light into a light spectrum that can be perceived by the human eye. A wide variety of colors can be produced depending on the composition of the gases. Transparent glass tubes are difficult to see by day and their effect is improved by coloring them.

Neon tubes are under a high voltage and using them in signage requires observation of the necessary safeguards and careful attention to installation instructions. The glass tubes have a diameter of between 8 and 30 millimeters and can be formed into almost any shape by trained glassblowers. Cursive and ornamental scripts in which the letters are interconnected are particularly well suited to neon signage. In the case of interruptions, such as with sans serif scripts, the connecting glass tube is painted to blend in with the substrate. Due to their aesthetic quality, freely formed neon signs remain in demand—particularly among artists. They are mounted directly onto the facade, placed in boxes open to the front, or mounted on three-dimensional letter shapes.

4.3

ILLUMINATED LETTERS

In the case of illuminated letters, the light source is mounted inside a three-dimensional body so that it is invisible from the outside. The aim is to achieve homogeneous illumination of the letter's surface. Older means of lighting, such as filament lamps and neon and fluorescent lamps, are still used today, but in most cases manufacturers opt for more energy-efficient and long-lasting LEDs. The lifespan of LEDs is dependent on the operating temperature and amounts to between 50,000 and 80,000 hours. The light intensity of LEDs is easily controllable, and can be adjusted over the course of a day and in accordance with official regulations. Light density (luminance) is measured in candela per square meter (cd/m^2).

With today's LED technology, very flat illuminated lettering (25–35 millimeters deep) can be produced that provides homogeneous illumination. These letters are milled from solid, multilayered acrylic glass and the LEDs are positioned in milled channels on the back side.

Letters with larger vertical heights, bar widths, and horizontal depths are constructed as hollow bodies with a front panel, back wall, and side sections. Formerly the sides were made of metal and the front panel from glass or plastic. Today, transparent, translucent, or opaque acrylic glass—in some cases aluminum—is used. In the case of very large letters, tensioned fabric is also used for the front panels.

The lighting effect is controlled in various ways and different lighting techniques can be combined. The light can be emitted from the front, sides, or back of letters; in the latter case, a shadow effect is created.

Colored LEDs are now being used less frequently. Dyed acrylic glass plates are available in a wide range of standard colors and plates can be specially dyed for large series. Cover sheeting or film is also available in many standard colors; special colors can be individually mixed and then plotted on the film that is glued to the acrylic glass. Illuminated letters can be covered with special films that make them appear black by day but glow white at night.

Every form of illuminated or animated external advertising requires an electricity supply and a control mechanism, which need to be taken into account in the design phase. In new buildings, illuminated letters can be supplied with electricity individually through the facade. In the case of existing buildings, double power rails are usually used that connect the letters with one another and help support them. Although these power rails are made as thin as possible and color-matched with the substrate, they seldom provide an aesthetically satisfactory solution. Fluorescent tubes and lamps and LEDs require appropriate ballasts and power supply units, the positioning of which needs to be included in the design. They can be installed inside or outside the illuminated form.

Illuminated signage can be mounted on roofs, which makes it particularly effective over a long distance. When installing such signage, it is important to ensure that the roof remains waterproof and that the signage is wind resistant. The supporting structures required here, which are in some cases solid, are not visible at night but are clearly so by day. They therefore constitute an integral part of the design process.

4.4 LIGHT BOXES

Light boxes are built in the same way as illuminated letters but exhibit a flat surface, which can be square, round, or oval. They are the self-illuminating counterpart to non-illuminated signs and are mounted flush onto facades or as right-angled projections, or are hung from projecting roofs.

Large-scale light boxes are often covered by tensioned fabric that needs to be extremely tear resistant. This fabric can be digitally printed with lettering or logos or used as a substrate for colored or lettered film.

In many cities, double-sided light boxes—as opposed to signage composed of individual letters—are no longer approved due to their major effect on the integrity of facades.

5.1 MECHANICALLY ANIMATED AND KINETIC SIGNAGE TYPES

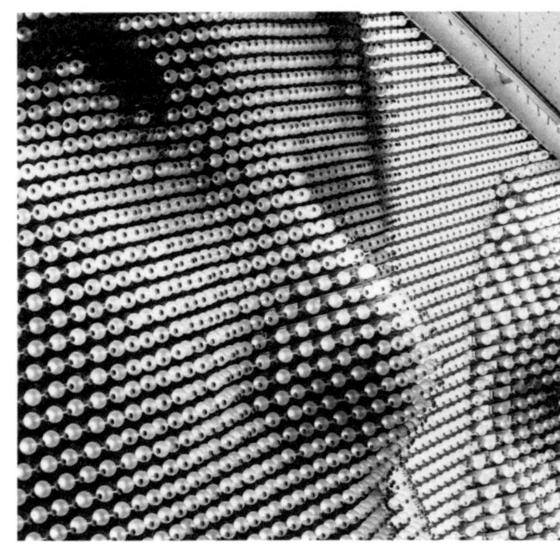

Mechanically moved objects in urban space attract particular attention and can be seen from different directions. Such installations feature individual letters, words, or symbols that are moved around a fixed axis by means of a motor. In the case of kinetic facades, digitally controllable rods or other elements simulate three-dimensional texts or images.

5.2

(ANIMATED) PROJECTIONS

Projected lettering, symbols, and images function ideally in twilight and can use entire buildings or landscapes as a screen. In most cases they are animated and used for temporary events. However, static uses—such as in the signaletics field—are also possible. Videos and texts can be projected onto large surfaces by high-performance beamers. Laser projections can be used to represent lines and contours but not surfaces; their advantage is that the content they project is visible over long distances. Projections are difficult to see by day, and their effect can be augmented by specials films applied to glass.

5.3

LED WALLS AND MEDIA FACADES

When controllable digital elements, such as LEDs, are symbiotically integrated into an entire facade surface, we speak of a media facade. LED installations over large areas in exterior and interior space are referred to as LED walls. The resolution of LED panels is measured in terms of pixel pitch, which is a measure of the distance from one diode to the next over a particular area: the smaller the pitch, the higher the resolution of the LED display and the better the quality of texts and images. LED panels for close-range uses have a pitch of between 5 and 8 millimeters; panels used in external space have a pitch of 16 millimeters or more. The luminance of an advertisement displayed in external space is approximately 8000 cd/m^2.

Every media facade and LED wall is centrally controlled by corresponding software referred to as a CMS.[9] The standard software available on the market is supplemented by modules that define the content, color, and degree of abstraction of motifs as well as the speed of movement and the way content is faded in and out. In some cases this results in a pleasing interplay between images/texts and architecture.

9 content management system

5.4

MONITORS / SCREENS

In most cases, prefabricated screens are installed in building envelopes and display windows and are (still) significantly cheaper than LED walls. In the case of LCD screens,[10] the orientation of liquid crystals is controlled by electronic impulses. Screens that are positioned in exterior space and designed for twenty-four-hour operation have a significantly higher luminance and lifespan than screens used in interior spaces. A recent development has seen the use of e-paper for signage on, for example, gas stations. While offering only two colors, this form of display is easy to read, including from the side and in bright sunlight. Above all, this technology requires significantly less energy than LCD screens.

The size, proportions, and positioning of screens are all factors that should be taken into account in the design process. Combining them with additional lighting installations simplifies their integration in facades and supplements their efficacy in twilight and at night.

10 liquid-crystal displays

PROJECT PARTICIPANTS AND PLANNING PHASES

The publication aims to promote a new awareness of the interfaces between architecture and graphic design and to contribute to a qualitative improvement of signage. Building signage works when it is integrally projected and implemented, and when the general framework in which it operates is a suitable one. What can the different stakeholders involved in the development of archigraphics contribute to this situation, and how can signage projects be ideally implemented?

PROJECT PARTICIPANTS

Municipalities
Building signage has an impact on public space. Municipal authorities develop and define locally specific design guidelines in collaboration with experts. These ensure—together with legal frameworks—a high quality of design in public space.

Building developers
Building developers (or their representatives) consider the need for building signage and incorporate it into planning specifications at an early stage in order to avoid undesirable retrofitting. They award direct commissions, conduct architect selection procedures, and—in the case of large building projects—hold competitions. Firms engaged to manage construction obtain offers from qualified graphic and signaletics design firms, which in turn engage appropriate manufacturers. Building developers ensure that, in the case of competitions, jury members have the necessary competence.

Architects and graphic designers
Depending on the competition tender/building project, architects engage the services of graphic designers or typographers—or vice versa. Architects and signage designers check the possibilities allowed by building regulations and develop their approaches taking the other specialism into consideration or working closely with its representatives. They also propose signage where they deem it appropriate even if competition organizers or the building developers have not requested it. Building signage needs to be budgeted for in both the design remuneration and the implementation costs. Integrating signage manufacturers into the planning process at an early stage facilitates innovative solutions and increases budget security.

Manufacturers
In the case of larger signage projects, manufacturers involve architects and designers at an early stage, both in the development of new technologies and in the development of new signage techniques and products. Conversely, architects and designers involve manufacturers in projects early on as consultants with extensive technical knowledge.

CHALLENGES FOR ARCHITECTS AND GRAPHIC DESIGNERS

Architects and graphic design
During their training, architects are not confronted with lettering and typography. They are therefore generally not acquainted with the different trajectories of development in the fields of graphic and lettering design or with the practical implementation possibilities available. With regard to choice of lettering, dimensioning, positioning, orientation, colors, materials, and layout, their best option is therefore to draw on the services of qualified graphic designers or typographers.

Graphic designers and spatial design
The challenge for graphic designers normally working in the two-dimensional field is engaging with the aesthetic and spatial-constructive principles of architecture. Graphic designers need to supplement their skills with regard to lettering selection, font design, and typographic and graphic design with additional knowledge. This includes informing themselves about materials and their specific features, different construction and montage processes, and construction-specific color systems such as RAL and NCS. The discipline of graphic design requires specific competences with regard to visualization, i.e., the mastering of image processing and 3D programs as well as model-building skills. Knowledge of different lighting and illumination techniques is also useful.

PLANNING PHASES

The processes involved in small and medium-sized signage projects can be structured into phases similar to those found in building projects. These are basically as follows:

Requirement analysis/planning

- Briefing: discussion with the client (building developer, architects) regarding the type of building, architectural design idea, built environment, spatial organization (exterior/interior), possible intervention locations, existing color and materials concepts, and nomenclature (room designations and numbering systems)
- Submission of existing plans, visualizations, renderings, model photography; clarification of competences and schedules
- Site inspection wherever possible in order to gain an impression of the spaces and dimensions and to check path layouts/lines of sight; organization of photographic documentation and/or historical photographs (in building-historical and other archives)

Preliminary study/design concept

- Establishment/analysis of basic framework: obtaining and checking building laws and guidelines from municipal authorities (incl. application forms, cadastral surveys). Clarification of particular conditions: Is the object located in the historic city center? Is it heritage-listed?
- Creation of a provisional signage register*: a hierarchically arranged register of all signage elements (main, incidental, floor and door signage, exterior and interior wayfinding elements, special signage) forms the basis of all further work steps. A provisional version is created in the first phase and supplemented in the course of the planning process.
- Design concept: development of overarching design ideas; font, color, dimensions, construction, and materials are planned and designed in parallel; visualization of variants and, where required, testing with models
- Visualization (Photoshop montages, 3D visualizations): presentation of different variants of ideas. The entire system must be clearly recognizable and an example solution presented for every element of the hierarchical chain of symbols. The presentation involves construction sketches, color and materials samples, and, depending on the project, handmade models.

Project planning/approval procedures

- Elaboration of and detail work on the selected design
- Definition of design, layout, and construction
- Where required, production of 1:1 samples
- Production of reference plan as basis for the submission

Submission/awarding contracts

- Compilation of submission documentation (quote requests)
- Obtaining and evaluation of offers from different potential contractors

Realization/montage

- Implementation planning for graphics/layout and construction
- Ongoing discussion and integration of changes up until final approval
- Preparation of all data (final drafting) and delivery to manufacturers
- Supervision of manufacture (layout, construction plans)
- Preparation of montage layouts; supervision of montage onsite
- Participation in approval inspection onsite by architects/building developer

Operation/maintenance

The final documentation serves to guarantee the maintenance of signage over the long term. It includes:

- the signage concept
- the signage register incl. photographic documentation of all elements
- the montage layouts and positioning plans
- the construction plans and graphic production data
- the addresses of all participating planners, developers, and manufacturers

The planning phases for comprehensive signage and signalization projects are more complex and have to be discussed and agreed with manufacturers on a case-by-case basis. A contract may be drawn up with manufacturers for the maintenance of larger advertising structures.

* The signage register is used to

- retain an overview of all signage elements
- help calculate the design fee
- produce submission documentation
- brief manufacturers
- provide technicians with an overview on site
- document projects

It contains:

- the official room number (as used in the plans)
- the identification of content (text/number/pictogram)
- information on bearing/base material (glass, concrete, painted wall, stele, etc.)
- type of signage (transparency, painting, screen print, metal letters, illuminated letters, etc.)
- type of installation (glued, screwed, assembled with spacers, etc.)

BIBLIOGRAPHY

Abbondandolo, Ilaria. *Carlo Scarpa è la Forma delle Parole.* Venice: Marsilio Editori, 2011.

Aicher, Otl. *Zeichensysteme der visuellen Kommunikation. Handbuch für Designer, Architekten, Planer, Organisatoren.* Berlin: Ernst & Sohn, 1996.

Ametov, Maria et al. *Building the Revolution: Soviet Art and Architecture, 1915–1935.* London: Royal Academy of Arts, 2011.

Archithese 1 (1995) – "Schrift am Bau – Calligraphie et facade.", Zurich: Niggli. 1/1995

Baines, Phil/Dixon, Catherine. *Signs: Lettering the Environment.* London: Laurence King Publishing Ltd, 2003.

Banham, Stephen. *Characters – Cultural stories revealed through typography.* Melbourne: Thames & Hudson, 2011.

Barthes, Roland. "Semiology and Urbanism." In Roland Barthes, *The Semiotic Challenge,* trans. Richard Howard, New York: Hill and Wang, 1988.

Bartram, Alan. *Lettering in Architecture.* London: Lund Humphries, 1975

Basheer Graphic Books. *Type Spaces – Typography in three-dimensional spaces.* Singapore: Basheer Graphic Books, 2013.

Bauer, Ewin K./Mayer, Dietrich (eds). *Orientation & Identity. Porträts internationaler Leitsysteme.* Vienna: Springer-Verlag, 2009.

Baumberger, Christoph. "Gebaute Zeichen. Zu den Bedeutungsweisen von Bauwerken." In Jörg Gleiter (ed.), *2014: Symptom Design. Vom Zeigen und Sich-Zeigen der Dinge.* Bielefeld: transkript, 2014.

Baur, Ruedi et al. *Das Gesetz und seine visuellen Folgen.* Baden: Lars Müller Publishers, 2005 *Construction. Design intégral Ruedi Baur & Associés.* Baden: Lars Müller Publishers, 1998.
Intégral Ruedi Baur et associés. Paris: Pyramid, 2003.
Antizipieren, Hinterfragen, Einschreiben, Irritieren, Orientieren, Übersetzen, Unterscheiden. Baden: Lars Müller Publishers, 2009.

Benevolo, Leonardo. *The History of the City.* Cambridge MA: MIT Press, 1990.

Benham, Reyner. *The Architecture of the Well-tempered Environment.* Chicago: University of Chicago Press, 1969.

Berliner Festspiele. *WChuTEMAS. Ein russisches Labor der Moderne – Architekturentwürfe 1920–1930.* Berlin: Berliner Festspiele, 2014.

Bignens, Christoph. *"Swiss style" – Die grosse Zeit der Gebrauchsgrafik in der Schweiz 1914–1964.* Zurich: Chronos, 2000.

Bignens, Christoph. *Kinos – Architektur als Marketing.* Zurich: Verlag Hans Rohr, 1988.

Bisani, Thomas. *Archigrafia – tra architettura e parola.* Triest: Università delli Studi di Trieste (2009, unpublished).

Berger, Craig. *Wayfinding. Designing and implementing graphic navigational systems.* Crans-Près-Céligny: RotoVision, 2005.

Boissière, Olivier. *Jean Nouvel, Emmanuel Cattani und Partner.* Zurich: Artemis Verlag, 1992.

Brook, Tony/Shaughnessy, Adrian. *Supergraphics – Transforming space: Graphic Design for Walls, Buildings & Spaces.* London: Unit Editions, 2010.

Collet, Emmanuel/Joosten, Christian/Pasquet, Denis/Parmentier, Isabelle/Vincke, Vincent. *De la pub plein les murs – Peintures murales et enseignes commerciales.* Brussels: Editions Racine, 2010.

de Fusco, Renato. *Architektur als Massenmedium. Anmerkungen zu einer Semiotik der gebauten Form.* Gütersloh: Bertelsmann, 1972.

Dempf, Rainer/Mattl, Siegfried/Steinbrener, Christoph (eds). *Delete! Die Entschriftung des öffentlichen Raums.* Freiburg im Breisgau: Orange Press, 2006.

Design Media Publishing Ltd. *Graphic Design in Architecture.* Hong Kong: Design Media Publishing Ltd, 2010.

Dexel, Walter. "Reklame im Stadtbilde." *Das neue Frankfurt. Monatsschrift für die Fragen der Großstadt-Gestaltung* 3 (1927).

Domesle, Andrea. *Leucht – Schrift – Kunst. Holzer, Kosuth, Nannucci, Nauman.* Berlin: Dietrich Reimer Verlag, 1998.

Draeger, Wolfgang: "Neon: der kalte Glamour der Urbanität." *Du: die Zeitschrift der Kultur* 5 (1981).

Eco, Umberto. *Einführung in die Semiotik.* Munich: UTB, 1972.

Estrada, Silvie. *SIGN.* Barcelona: Index Book, 2012.

Evans, Walker. *Signs.* London: Thames and Hudson Ltd, 1998.

Feuerhorst, Ulrich/Steinle, Holger: "Emailplakate – Geschichte, Herstellung, Anbringungsorte." *Du: Zeitschrift der Kultur* 4 (1983).

Fleischmann, Gerd. *bauhaus – drucksachen typografie reklame.* Düsseldorf: edition marzona, 1984.

Foges, Chris. *Outsize – Large Scale Graphic Design.* Mies: Rotovision SA, 2003.

Fonds d'art contemporain de la Ville de Genève. *Neon Parallax Genève 2006–2012.* Gollion: Infolio Editions, 2012.

Follis, John/Hammer, Dave. *Architectural signing and graphics.* London: Architectural Press, 1979.

FVL, Fachverband für Lichtwerbung e.V. *Signaturen der Nacht - Die Welt der Lichtwerbung.* Ludwigsburg: avedition GmbH, 2009.

Galindo, Michelle. *Signage Design.* Cincinnati: Braun Publishing AG, 2012.

Gärtner, Ulrike/Hemken Kai-Uwe/Schierz Kai-Uwe. *Kunst Licht Spiele.* Bielefeld: Kerber Verlag, 2009.

Gray, Nicolete. *Lettering on buildings.* London: Architectural Press, 1960.

Haas, Cynthia Lea. *Ghost Signs of Arkansas.* Fayetteville: University of Arkansas Press, 1997.

Haenzer, Markus. *Krieg der Zeichen. Spurenlesen im urbanen Raum.* Mainz: Verlag Hermann Schmidt, 2009.

Heller, Steven/Ilic, Mirko. *Lettering Large – Art and design of monumental typography.* New York: The Monacelli Press, 2013.

Hellweg, Werner. *Die Außenreklame in Stadt und Land.* Hamburg: Verlag Konrad Hans, 1919.

Hemken, Kai-Uwe. *El Lissitzky. Revolution und Avantgarde.* Cologne: DuMont, 1990.

Henke, Silvia/Lichtenstein, Claude (eds). *Gebäude – Schrift – Signal.* Zurich: Kontrast, 2005.

Henkin, David M. *City Reading – Written Words and Public Spaces in Antebellum New York.* New York: Columbia University Press, 1998.

Herdeg, Walter. *Archigraphia – Architektur- und Signalisierungsgraphik.* Zurich: Graphis Press, 1978.

Hollis, Richard. *Graphic Design – A concise history.* London: Thames & Hudson, 2001.
Swiss Graphic Design – The Origins and Growth of an International Style 1920–1965. London: Laurence King Publishing Ltd, 2006.

Hochschule für Grafik und Kunst Leipzig. *Architektur und Grafik.* Baden: Lars Müller Publishers, 1998.

Hoormann, Anne. *Lichtspiel, zur Medienreflexion der Avantgarde der Weimarer Republik.* Munich: Wilhelm Fink Verlag, 2003.

Internationales Städteforum in Graz. *Die umworbene Stadt. Stadtgestalt und Werbung im Fokus von Denkmalpflege und Baukultur.* Graz: Universitätsdruckerei Klampfer GmbH, 2013.

Jencks, Charles. *The Language of Post-Modern Architecture.* New York: Rizzoli, 1977.

Johnston, Edward. *Writing – Illuminating – Lettering.* London: John Hog, 1906.

Jury, David. *Graphic Design before Graphic Designers – The Printer as Designer and Craftsman 1700–1914.* London: Thames & Hudson, 2012.

Kinneir, Jock. *Words and Buildings: The Art and Practice of Public Lettering.* London: The Architectural Press Ltd, 1980.

Karwinska, Ilona. *Polish Cold War Neon.* New York: Mark Batty Publisher, 2009.

Kling, Beate/Torsten Krüger (eds). *Signaletik – Orientierung im Raum.* Munich: DETAIL, 2013.

Klotz, Heinrich (ed.). *Venturi, Robert – Komplexität und Widerspruch in der Architektur* (1978). Basel: Birkhäuser, 2000.

Kohlhaas, Rem. *S, M, L, XL.* New York: The Monacelli Press, 1998.
Delirious New York. New York: The Monacelli Press, 1994.

Kracauer, Siegfried. *Das Ornament der Masse.* Frankfurt a. M.: Suhrkamp, 1963
Kreutzer, Dietmar. *Werbung im Stadtraum.* Berlin: Verlag für Bauwesen, 1995
Kübler, Christof. *Wider den hermetischen Zauber. Rationalistische Erneuerung alpiner Architektur um 1930. Rudolf Gaberel und Davos.* Chur: Verlag Bündner Monatsblatt/Desertina AG, 1997.
Linke, Oliver. *Von Asam bis Zrenner – Auf den Spuren des Münchner Schriftenmalers Karl Blaschke.* Munich: August Dreesbach Verlag, 2013.
Loos, Adolf. "Ornament als Verbrechen." In Adolf Loos, *Sämtliche Schriften,* Vienna: Verlagsgesellschaft m.b.h, 1908.
Lynch, Kevin. *The Image of the City.* Cambridge: MIT Press, 1960.
Mack, Gerhard. *Herzog & de Meuron 1978–1988.* Basel: Birkhäuser, 1997.
Herzog & de Meuron 1989–1991. Basel: Birkhäuser, 1996.
Herzog & de Meuron 1992–1996. Basel: Birkhäuser, 2000.
Mahar, Lisa. *American Signs. Form and Meaning on Route 66.* New York: The Monacelli Press, 2002.
Mataja, Victor. *Die Reklame.* Berlin/Leipzig: Duncker und Humboldt, 1909/1920.
May, Ernst: "Städtebeau und Lichtreklame." In Wilhelm Lotz (ed.), *Licht und Beleuchtung,* Berlin: Verlag Hermann Reckendorf, 1928.
Meier-Menzel, Hans-Jürgen. *Schrift + Zeichen am Bau.* Munich: Callwey, 1961.
Mendelssohn, Erich. *Amerika. Bilderbuch eines Architekten.* Berlin: Mosse, 1926 (reprinted 1992 Braunschweig: Vieweg).
Meuser, Philipp/Pogade, Daniela. *Raumzeichen. Architektur und Kommunikations-Design.* Berlin: DOM-publishers, 2005.
Mollerup, Per. *Wayshowing. A Guide to Environmental Signage: Principles & Practices.* Baden, Lars Müller Publishers, 2004.
Müller, Lars. *Josef-Müller Brockmann.* Baden: Lars Müller Publishers, 1996.
Müller-Brockmann, Josef. *Gestaltungsprobleme des Grafikers – Gestalterische und erzieherische Probleme in der Werbegrafik – die Ausbildung des Grafikers.* Sulgen: Niggli, 1961 (2003).
Murray, James T./Murray, Karla L. *Store Front – The Disappearing Face of New York.* Berkeley: Gingko Press Inc., 2008.
Naegele, Isabel/Baur, Ruedi. *Scents of the City. Aroma der Stadt.* Baden: Lars Müller Publishers, 2004.
Nentwig, Franziska (ed.). *Berlin im Licht.* Berlin: Stiftung Stadtmuseum Berlin, 2008.
Nettelhorst, Leopold. *Außenwerbung, Werbung am Bau und im öffentlichen Raum.* Munich: Callwey, 1952.
Plaste und Elaste – Leuchtreklame in der DDR. Berlin: Neues Leben Verlag, 2010.
Oechslin, Werner: "Architektur und Alphabet." In Braegger, Carlpeter (eds), *Architektur und Sprache,* Munich: Prestel, 1982, 216–254.
Stilhülse und Kern – Otto Wagner, Adolf Loos und der evolutionäre Weg zur modernen Architektur. Zurich: ETH, 1994.
"Lichtarchitektur." In *Moderne Architektur in Deutschland 1900–1950.* Frankfurt a. M.: Architekturmuseum Frankfurt, 1994, 116–129.
Petrucci, Armando. *Public Lettering. Script, Power, and Culture.* Chicago/London: The University of Chicago Press, 1993.
La scrittura: Ideologia e rappresentazione. Turin: Giulio Einaudi editore s.p.a., 1980 (1986).
Poulin, Richard. *Graphic Design and Architecture. A 20th Century History: A Guide to Type, Image, Symbol and Visual Storytelling in the Modern World.* Beverly: Rockport Publishers, 2012.
Powelichina, Alla/Kowtun, Jewgeni. *Das russische Reklameschild und die Künste der Avantgarde.* Leningrad: Aurora-Kunstverlag, 1991.
Pro Message Kommunikation und Medien. *Sehnsüchte: Lichtreklame in den 50er Jahren: Fotografien aus dem Studio Bergerhausen.* Ludwigshafen am Rhein: Pro Message Kommunikation und Medien, 2001.
Reinhardt, Ernst. "Gestaltung der Lichtreklame." *Die Form* 4 (1929).
Ribbat, Christoph. *Flackernde Moderne – Die Geschichte des Neonlichts.* Stuttgart: Franz Steiner Verlag, 2011.
Rinaldi, Thomas E. *New York Neon.* New York/London: W. W. Norton & Company, 2013.
Rykwert, Joseph. *Ornament ist kein Verbrechen – Architektur als Kunst.* Cologne: DuMont Buchverlag, 1983.
Schwitters, Kurt. *Typografie und Werbegestaltung.* Wiesbaden: Museum Wiesbaden, 1990.
Slanted Magazine 18 (2012) – "Signage – Orientation."
Saccani, Anna. *La ville en toutes lettres – Installations typographiques dans l'espace public.* London: Thames & Hudson Ltd/Rome: SHS Publishing, 2013.
Schmed, Silvio/Kübler, Christof. *Reklameanalyse Innenstadt Zürich – Die Dominanz der Mittelmässigkeit.* Zurich: Amt für Städtebau, 1995 (unpublished study).
Sennett, Richard. *Civitas. Die Großstadt und die Kultur des Unterschieds.* Frankfurt a. M.: Fischer Verlag, 1983.
Schmidt-Brümmer, Horst. *Wandmalerei zwischen Reklamekunst, Phantasie und Protest.* Cologne: DuMont, 1982.
Smith, Virginia. *Forms in Modernism – A Visual Set.* New York: Watson-Guptill Publications, 2005.
Smitshuijzen, Edo. *Signage Design Manual.* Baden: Lars Müller Publishers, 2007.
Sprengnagel, Dusty. *Neon World.* Cincinnatti: ST Publications, Inc., 1999.
Stadler, Hilar/Stierli, Martino. *Bilder aus dem Archiv von Robert Venturi und Denise Scott Brown.* Zurich: Scheidegger & Spiess, 2008.
Stadt Zürich, Amt für Städtebau. *Reklame im Stadtbild – Gebäudebeschriftung, Lichtreklame und Plakatierung und Zürich.* Zurich: Amt für Städtebau, 2009.
Stern, Rudi. *Let there be Neon.* Cincinnati: ST Publications, Inc., 1979.
Stierli, Martino. Las *Vegas im Rückspiegel. Die Stadt in Theorie, Fotografie und Film.* Zurich: gta Verlag, 2010 (dissertation).
Sutton, James. *Signs in action.* London: Studio Vista/New York: Reinhold Publishing Corporation, 1965.
Tell, Darcy. *Times Square Spectacular – Lighting up Broadway.* New York: Smithsonian Books, 2007.
The Society for Environmental Graphic Design (SEGD). *You Are Here. Graphics That Direct, Explain & Entertain.* Cincinnatti: ST Publications, 1999.
Two Point.Net. *Left, Right, Up, Down – Neue Ansätze für die Gestaltung von Leitsystemen.* Berlin: Gestalten, 2010.
Uebele, Andreas. *Schrift im Raum. Visuelle Kommunikation und Architektur.* Mainz: Verlag Hermann Schmidt, 2000.
Venturi, Robert. *Complexity and Contradiction in Architecture.* New York: Museum of Modern Art, 1966.
Venturi, Robert/Scott Brown, Denise/Izenour, Steve. *Learning from Las Vegas.* Cambridge MA: MIT Press, 1977 (revised edition).
Venturi, Robert/Scott Brown Denise. *Architecture as Signs and Systems – For a Mannerist Time.* Cambridge, Massachusetts/London: Harvard University Press, 2004.
Vogt, Adolf Max. *Russische und französische Revolutionsarchitektur 1917–1789.* Braunschweig/Wiesbaden: Friedr. Vieweg & Sohn, 1974 (1990).
von Moos, Stanislaus. *Venturi and Rauch – Architektur im Alltag Amerikas.* Zurich: Kunstgewerbemuseum, 1979.
Venturi, Rauch & Scott Brown. Munich: Schirmer-Mosel, 1987.
Wanetzky, Harald. *Typotektur – Architektur und Typografie im 20. Jahrhundert. Der Modellfall einer Zusammenführung.* Universität Freiburg im Breisgau, 1995 (dissertation).

Wenzel, Patrick. *Handbuch Beschilderungsplanung. Planungshilfen für die Konzeption von Fußgänger-Leitsystemen.* Hünstetten: Patrick Wenzel, 2003.
Wolfe, Tom. "Electrographic Architecture." *Architectural Design* (July 1969): 380–382.
Zec, Peter. *Orientierung im Raum – Eine Untersuchung zur Gestaltung von Orientierungs- und Leitsystemen,* Essen: MABEG, 2002.

AUTHOR PORTRAITS

Agnès Laube
Born in 1964 in Lengnau/AG, lives in Zurich. Graphic designer, lecturer, and author. Studied graphic design 1984–89 at the Zurich School of Art and Design (now Zurich University of the Arts). Worked with Pierre Miedinger, Zurich. Since 1991, has had her own studio in Zurich. Since 2003, guest lecturer at different art schools in Switzerland (including HSLU/Design & Art in Lucerne and the University of the Arts in Berne). From 2011 to 2015, head of the Communication Design MA course at the University of the Arts in Berne. Since February 2015, has worked freelance again as a designer, consultant, and journalist, and with firms and institutions in Switzerland and abroad.

Michael Widrig
Born in 1966 in Pratteln/BL, lives in Zurich. Architect. Studied at the ETH Zurich. Worked with Gigon/Guyer Architekten. Own office since 1998. Diverse associate lecturer positions at the ETH Zurich and the EPFL Lausanne. In 2013–14, lecturer at the University of the Arts in Berne. Since 2003, has shared architecture office with Daniel Kaufmann (Kaufmann Widrig Architekten GmbH).

Since 2003, the two authors have worked, taught, researched, curated, and published around the theme of archigraphy (www.archigrafie.ch).

PICTURE CREDIT

Part 1: Introduction

1 UNESCO-World Heritage Fagus-Werk, Alfeld
2 Bauhaus-Archiv, Berlin
3 Wikimedia Commons, CC BY-NC-SA 4.0
4 Wikimedia Commons, Spyros Drakopoulos, CC BY-SA 4.0,
5 Baugeschichtliches Archiv, Zurich
6 Creative Commons BY-SA
7 Bauhaus-Archiv, Berlin
8 Bauhaus-Archiv, Berlin
9 Tretyakov-Gallery, Moscow
10 Merrill C. Berman Collection, New York
11 Wikimedia Commons, Andrey Kryuchenko, CC BY-SA 3.0
12 Museum of Modern Art/Scala, Florenz
13 Ministère de la Culture – Médiathèque du Patrimoine, Paris
14 Creative Commons, Sara Burns, CC BY-NC-SA 4.0
15 Akademie der Künste, Berlin
16 Akademie der Künste, Berlin
17 Akademie der Künste, Berlin
18 Akademie der Künste, Berlin
19 Baugeschichtliches Archiv, Zurich
20 Wikimedia Commons, CC BY-NC-SA 4.0
21 Theodor Stalder, Zurich
22 Danmark Kunstbibliotek, Copenhagen
23 angela thomas schmid/pro litteris, Zurich
24 Baugeschichtliches Archiv, Zurich
25 Wikimedia Commons, CC BY-NC-SA 4.0
26 Georg Krähenbühl, Davos
27 Museum für Gestaltung Zurich, Graphics Collection
28 archiv max bill, binia + jakob bill stiftung, Zurich
29 Baugeschichtliches Archiv, Zurich
30 Baugeschichtliches Archiv, Zurich
31 Wikimedia Commons, CC BY-NC-SA 4.0
32 Wikimedia Commons, CC BY-NC-SA 4.0
33 Baugeschichtliches Archiv, Zurich
34 Baugeschichtliches Archiv, Zurich
35 Archive of Henkel & Co., KGaA, Düsseldorf
36 Wikimedia Commons, CC BY-NC-SA 4.0
37 Baugeschichtliches Archiv, Zurich
38 Museum für Gestaltung Zurich, Graphics Collection
39 Theodor Stalder, Zurich
40 Baugeschichtliches Archiv, Zurich
41 Fondazione nazionale per la tutela, la conservazione e la gestione dei Beni di interesse storico, artistico e naturalistico, Milan
42 Venturi Scott Brown and Ass. (VSBA), Tom Bernard
43 VSBA, Tom Bernard
44 Wikimedia Commons, CC BY-NC-SA 4.0
45 VSBA, William Watkins
46 SITE Architects, New York
47 SITE Architects, New York
48 VSBA, Stephen Hill
49 Wikimedia Commons, CC BY-NC-SA 4.0
50 Jean-Philippe Lenclos, Paris
51 SITE Architects, New York
52 Jerry Cinamon, London
53 Sussman/Prejza, Los Angeles
54 Jean-Philippe Lenclos, Paris
55 Jean-Philippe Lenclos, Paris
56 Barbara Stauffacher Solomon, San Francisco
57 Barbara Stauffacher Solomon, San Francisco
58 Jean-Philippe Lenclos, Paris
59 Barbara Burg + Oliver Schuh, Cologne
60 Herzog & de Meuron, Basel
61 Ateliers Jean Nouvel, Paris
62 Gaston Bergeret, Paris
63 Ruedi Walti, Basel
64 Transform GmbH, Wettingen
65 Herzog & de Meuron, Basel
66 Heinrich Helfenstein, Zurich
67 HinderSchlatterFeuz, Zurich
68 Stephan Rutz, Zurich
69 Heinrich Helfenstein, Zurich
70 Christoph T. Hunziker, Birmensdorf
71 Mayo Bucher, Zurich
72 Georg Aerni, Zurich
73 VSBA, Matt Wargo
74 Scagliola/Brakkee, Rotterdam
75 Hild and K, Munich
76 Wikimedia Commons, CC BY-NC-SA 4.0
77 Westiform AG, Niederwangen-Bern
78 Westiform AG, Niederwangen-Bern
79 realities:united, Bernd Hiepe, Berlin
80 realities:united, Berlin
81 Wikimedia Commons, CC BY-NC-SA 4.0
82 VSBA, Philadelphia
83 VSBA, Philadelphia
84 Wikimedia Commons, CC BY-NC-SA 4.0,
85 Baugeschichtliches Archiv, Zurich
86 Wikimedia Commons, CC BY-NC-SA 4.0
87 Leonardo Finotti, São Paolo
88 Wikimedia Commons, CC BY-NC-SA 4.0
89 Baugeschichtliches Archiv, Zurich
90 Wikimedia Commons, CC BY-NC-SA 4.0
91 Baugeschichtliches Archiv, Zurich

Part 2: Case Studies

p. 45 Stefano Graziani, Triest
p. 46 top left and right: iart, Basel; bottom: Stefano Graziani, Triest
p. 47 Stefano Graziani, Triest
p. 49 Christian Richters, Berlin
p. 50 Ruedi Walti, Basel
p. 51 Ruedi Walti, Basel
p. 53 Michel Denancé, Paris
p. 54 top left: Michel Denancé, Paris; top right; bottom left and right: Renzo Piano Building Workshop, Genoa
p. 55 Michel Denancé, Paris
p. 57 Gehry Partners, LLP, Los Angeles
p. 58 Gehry Partners, LLP, Los Angeles
p. 59 Gehry Partners, LLP, Los Angeles
p. 61 bildbau gmbh, Zurich
p. 63 Herzog & de Meuron, Basel
p. 65 Leonardo Finotti, São Paulo
p. 66 top left: Franz Rindlisbacher, Zurich; top right: Velvet, Luzern; bottom: Leonardo Finotti, São Paulo
p. 67 Franz Rindlisbacher, Zurich
p. 69 Michael Heinrich, Munich
p. 71 João Ferrand, Matosinhos
p. 72 João Ferrand, Matosinhos
p. 73 João Ferrand, Matosinhos
p. 75 Emilio Photoimagination, M. Ridwan Kamil
p. 76 Emilio Photoimagination, M. Ridwan Kamil
p. 77 Emilio Photoimagination, M. Ridwan Kamil
p. 79 Dianna Snape, St. Kilda
p. 81 Roger Frei, Zurich
p. 82 top: Roger Frei, Zurich; bottom: bivgrafik, Zurich
p. 83 top right and left; bottom right: bivgrafik, Zurich; bottom left: Roger Frei, Zurich
p. 85 Niklaus Spoerri, Zurich
p. 86 top; bottom left: Niklaus Spoerri, Zurich bottom right: bivgrafik, Zurich
p. 87 top left, bottom left and right: Niklaus Spoerri, Zurich; top right: bivgrafik, Zurich
p. 89 Heinrich Helfenstein, Zurich
p. 91 Studio Marco Vermeulen, Rotterdam
p. 92 Studio Marco Vermeulen, Rotterdam
p. 93 Studio Marco Vermeulen, Rotterdam
p. 95 Arge Laube, Kaufmann Widrig, Zurich
p. 96 Arge Laube, Kaufmann Widrig, Zurich
p. 97 Arge Laube, Kaufmann Widrig, Zurich
p. 99 Hauser, Schwarz, Basel
p. 100 Hauser, Schwarz, Basel
p. 101 Hauser, Schwarz, Basel
p. 103 Theodor Stalder, Zurich
p. 104 Theodor Stalder, Zurich
p. 105 Theodor Stalder, Zurich
p. 107 Mark Röthlisberger, Zurich
p. 108 top: Mark Röthlisberger, Zurich; bottom: bivgrafik, Zurich
p. 109 bottom left: Mark Röthlisberger, Zurich; top left and right; bottom right: bivgrafik, Zurich
p. 111 Roland Bernath, Zurich
p. 113 Erick Saillet, Lyon
p. 114 Erick Saillet, Lyon
p. 115 Marie-Caroline Lucat, Montpellier
p. 117 Galeries Lafayette, Berlin
p. 118 Hélène Binet, London
p. 121 Theodor Stalder, Zurich
p. 122 Theodor Stalder, Zurich; bottom right: Hi – Visuelle Gestaltung, Luzern
p. 123 Theodor Stalder, Zurich
p. 125 Duccio Malagamba, Barcelona
p. 126 Duccio Malagamba, Barcelona
p. 127 Erica Overmeer, Amsterdam
p. 129 SITE Architects, New York
p. 131 intégral Ruedi Baur, Paris

p. 132 top: James Ewing, New York;
bottom: Intégral Ruedi Baur, Paris
p. 133 top left and right; bottom left: James Ewing, New York; bottom right: Intégral Ruedi Baur, Paris
p. 135 Theodor Stalder, Zurich
p. 136 Theodor Stalder, Zurich
p. 137 Georg Aerni, Zurich

Part 3: Appendix

1.1 top: Arge Laube, Kaufmann Widrig, Zurich;
centre: Theodor Stalder, Zurich;
bottom: Fondazione nazionale per la tutela, la conservazione e la gestione dei Beni di interesse storico, artistico e naturalistico, Milan
1.2 top: Theodor Stalder, Zurich;
bottom: Michael Heinrich, Munich;
1.3 top: Theodor Stalder, Zurich;
bottom: Manfred Seidl, Vienna
1.4 top: Arge Laube, Kaufmann Widrig, Zurich;
bottom: Theodor Stalder, Zurich
1.5 top: Theodor Stalder, Zurich;
bottom: Margherita Spiluttini, Vienna
2.1 top: Theodor Stalder, Zurich;
bottom: Stephan Banz, Cully
2.2 top: Emilio Photoimagination;
bottom: Dianna Snape, St. Kilda
2.3 Theodor Stalder, Zurich
3.1 top: Arge Laube, Kaufmann Widrig, Zurich;
bottom: Christoph T. Hunziker, Birmensdorf
3.2 Theodor Stalder, Zurich
3.3 intégral Ruedi Baur, Paris
3.4 bivgrafik, Zurich
3.5 top: bivgrafik, Zurich;
bottom: Arge Laube, Kaufmann Widrig, Zurich
3.6 top: João Ferrand, Matosinhos;
bottom: Theodor Stalder, Zurich
3.7 Westiform, Niederwangen-Bern
3.8 top: Theodor Stalder, Zurich;
bottom: Arge Laube, Kaufmann Widrig, Zurich
3.9 Arge Laube, Kaufmann Widrig, Zurich
3.10 Theodor Stalder, Zurich
3.11 top: Arge Laube, Kaufmann Widrig, Zurich;
bottom: Theodor Stalder, Zurich
3.12 Arge Laube, Kaufmann Widrig, Zurich
3.13 top: Chermayeff & Geismar & Haviv, New York;
bottom: Theodor Stalder, Zurich
4.1 top: Arge Laube, Kaufmann Widrig, Zurich;
bottom: Theodor Stalder, Zurich
4.2 top: Westiform, Bern-Niederwangen;
centre: Theodor Stalder, Zurich;
bottom: Theodor Stalder, Zurich
4.3 Theodor Stalder, Zurich
4.4 top: Theodor Stalder, Zurich;
bottom: Hannes Henz, Zurich
5.1 top: Stephan Banz, Cully;
bottom: iart, Asif Khan, Basel
5.2 Stéphane Dabrowski, Paris
5.3 top: Theodor Stalder, Zurich;
bottom: realities:united, Bernd Hiepe, Berlin
5.4 realities:united, Berlin

MAIN SPONSOR

Westiform

For over half a century, Westiform has been making brands and companies shine worldwide. Advice to designers and architects for mounting lettering onto buildings is one of the core competences of this Swiss company, where for many years the typographer Adrian Frutiger was involved on the Supervisory Board. In addition to signage and branding, Westiform is also an expert in digital signage solutions, facade cladding, directional signage and POS solutions. In addition, Westiform is known for its use of state-of-the-art technology, professional advice, optimized processes and its customer-oriented style. Westiform is also environmentally driven and has an engineering department, which integrates energy efficient solutions into all of its products, which set standards within the industry. Westiform is a family owned business in its second generation.

westiform
visual communication

www.westiform.com
www.facebook.com/westiform
https://twitter.com/Westiform
https://www.linkedin.com/company/westiform-ag
https://www.xing.com/companies/westiformag

IMPRINT

Archigraphy – Lettering on Buildings
Agnès Laube, Michael Widrig

Concept and texts:
Agnès Laube, Michael Widrig
Translation:
Joe O'Donnell
Mark Kyburz (p. 52, 56, 70, 74, 78, 90, 112, 116, 118, 128)
Copy editing:
John Sweet
Project management:
Alexander Felix, Katharina Kulke
Production:
Amelie Solbrig
Layout and cover design:
Büro 146. Valentin Hindermann, Madeleine Stahel, Maike Hamacher, Zürich with Tiziana Artemisio
Typesetting:
Kathleen Bernsdorf

Paper:
Fly 07, 130 gr/m²
Printing:
DZA Druckerei zu Altenburg GmbH

Library of Congress Cataloging-in-Publication data:
A CIP catalog record for this book has been applied for at the Library of Congress.

Bibliographic information published by the German National Library
The German National Library lists this publication in the Deutsche Nationalbibliografie; detailed bibliographic data are available on the Internet at http://dnb.dnb.de.

This publication is also available as an e-book (ISBN PDF 978-3-0356-0555-6) and in a German language edition (ISBN 978-3-0356-0567-9).

P. O. Box 44, 4009 Basel, Switzerland
Part of Walter de Gruyter GmbH, Berlin/Boston

Printed on acid-free paper produced from chlorine-free pulp. TCF ∞
Printed in Germany

ISBN 978-3-0356-0568-6

9 8 7 6 5 4 3 2 1
www.birkhauser.com